Prepared in cooperation with the Task Force for Business and Stability Operations, under the auspices of the U.S. Department of Defense and the Afghanistan Geological Survey

Rare Earth Element Mineralogy, Geochemistry, and Preliminary Resource Assessment of the Khanneshin Carbonatite Complex, Helmand Province, Afghanistan

Robert D. Tucker, Harvey E. Belkin, Klaus J. Schulz, Stephen G. Peters, and Kim P. Buttleman

Open-File Report 2011–1207
USGS Afghanistan Project Product No. 200

U.S. Department of the Interior
U.S. Geological Survey

U.S. Department of the Interior
KEN SALAZAR, Secretary

U.S. Geological Survey
Marcia K. McNutt, Director

U.S. Geological Survey, Reston, Virginia: 2011

For more information on the USGS—the Federal source for science about the Earth, its natural and living resources, natural hazards, and the environment—visit *http://www.usgs.gov* or call 1–888–ASK–USGS

For an overview of USGS information products, including maps, imagery, and publications, visit *http://www.usgs.gov/pubprod*

To order this and other USGS information products, visit *http://store.usgs.gov*

Suggested citation:
Tucker, R.D., Belkin, H.E., Schulz, K.J., Peters, S.G., and Buttleman, K.P., 2011, Rare earth element mineralogy, geochemistry, and preliminary resource assessment of the Khanneshin carbonatite complex, Helmand Province, Afghanistan: U.S. Geological Survey Open-File Report 2011–1207, 50 p.

Contents

Figures

Tables

Conversion Factors

Multiply	By	To obtain
Length		
centimeter (cm)	0.3937	inch (in.)
millimeter (mm)	0.03937	inch (in.)
micrometer (μm)	0.0003937	inch (in.)
meter (m)	3.281	foot (ft)
kilometer (km)	0.6214	mile (mi)
meter (m)	1.094	yard (yd)
Area		
square meter (m^2)	0.0002471	acre
square kilometer (km^2)	247.1	acre
square centimeter (cm^2)	0.001076	square foot (ft^2)
square meter (m^2)	10.76	square foot (ft^2)
square centimeter (cm^2)	0.1550	square inch (ft^2)
square kilometer (km^2)	0.3861	square mile (mi^2)
Volume		
cubic centimeter (cm^3)	0.06102	cubic inch (in^3)
cubic meter (m^3)	35.31	cubic foot (ft^3)
cubic meter (m^3)	1.308	cubic yard (yd^3)
cubic kilometer (km^3)	0.2399	cubic mile (mi^3)
Mass		
gram (g)	0.03527	ounce, avoirdupois (oz)
kilogram (kg)	2.205	pound avoirdupois (lb)
metric ton (t)	1.1023	short ton (2,000 lbs)
million metric tons (Mt)	1.1023	million short tons
Density		
gram per cubic centimeter (g/cm^3)	62.4220	pound per cubic foot (lb/ft^3)

Temperature in degrees Celsius (°C) may be converted to degrees Fahrenheit (°F) as follows:
°F=(1.8×°C)+32

Rare Earth Element Mineralogy, Geochemistry, and Preliminary Resource Assessment of the Khanneshin Carbonatite Complex, Helmand Province, Afghanistan

Robert D. Tucker, Harvey E. Belkin, Klaus J. Schulz, Stephen G. Peters, and Kim P. Buttleman

Abstract

The Khanneshin carbonatite is a deeply dissected igneous complex of Quaternary age that rises approximately 700 meters (m) above the Neogene sedimentary rocks of the Registan Desert, Helmand Province, Afghanistan. The complex consists almost exclusively of carbonate-rich intrusive and extrusive igneous rocks, crudely circular in outline, with three small hypabyssal plugs of leucite phonolite and leucitite outcropping in the southeast part of the complex. The igneous complex is broadly divisible into a central intrusive vent (or massif), approximately 4 kilometers (km) in diameter, consisting of coarse-grained sövite and brecciated and agglomeratic barite-ankerite alvikite; a thin marginal zone (<1 km wide) of outwardly dipping (5°–45°) and alkali metasomatized Neogene sedimentary strata; and a peripheral apron of volcanic and volcaniclastic strata extending another 3–5 km away from the central intrusive vent. Small satellitic intrusions of biotite-calcite carbonatite and rare leucite phonolite, no larger than 400 m in diameter, crop out on the southern and southeastern margin of the central intrusive vent.

A zone of prospective light rare earth element (LREE) enrichment was delineated by Soviet geological teams in the mid-1970s. The area of LREE-enrichment is situated in extensively veined and dike-intruded barite-ankerite alvikite in the outer part of the central vent near its northeast contact with Neogene sedimentary rocks. In addition to having very high concentrations of LREE, the barite-ankerite alvikites are also highly enriched in barium and strontium.

Three reconnaissance scoping missions to the Khanneshin carbonatite were led by scientists of the U.S. Geological Survey (USGS). Two of these were to LREE area of interest which is the primary subject of this report.

Two types of LREE mineralization occur. Type-1 LREE mineralization consists of semiconcordant, symmetrically banded veins and discontinuous seams, as much as 0.5–0.7 m thick and several tens of meters long. These occur throughout a vertical thickness of at least 150 m. Type-1 banded veins and seams are yellow-weathering zones, symmetric about a dark central zone, that are enriched in khanneshite-(Ce), barite, strontianite, and secondary LREE minerals (synchysite-(Ce) and parisite-(Ce)). The dark central zone, consisting primarily of ankeritic dolomite, barite, apatite, and strontianite, also has trace khanneshite-(Ce). These type-1 veins and seams alternate with dark, meter-thick layers of ankerite-barite alvikite (wall rock) over a vertical distance of approximately 150 m. In some veins LREE carbonate minerals form dense spherically shaped aggregates (100 micrometers diameter), presumably crystallized from immiscible droplets, which constitute as much as 30 percent (by volume) of the vein. Type-1 veins and seams average 19.92 weight percent (wt. percent) Ba, 3.61 wt. percent Sr, and 2.78 wt. percent total LREE. The values of $\sum$ LREE ($\sum$ LREE is the sum of La, Ce, Pr, and Nd) for eight average whole-rocks range from 6.23 to 1.83 wt. percent.

Type-2 LREE mineralization occurs in discordant dikes and tabular sheets, as much as tens of meters wide and hundreds of meters long, which are composed of primary igneous minerals that crystallized directly from magma or a late-stage hydrothermal fluid. Type-2 discordant dikes are of two types—those enriched in fluorine, and those enriched in phosphorus. The igneous rocks enriched in fluorine have as their LREE-bearing minerals idiomorphic phenocrysts of khanneshite-(Ce) and monazite-(Ce), together with synchysite-(Ce), bastnäsite-(Ce), and calkinsite-(Ce) of likely secondary (late hydrothermal) origin. The igneous rocks enriched in phosphorus have as their LREE-enriched bearing minerals idiomorphic phenocrysts of carbocernaite, together with parisite-(Ce) of secondary origin. The type-2 LREE–enriched discordant dikes average 11.1 wt. percent Ba, 5.36 wt. percent Sr, and 3.28 wt. percent $\sum$ LREE. The values for $\sum$ LREE of fourteen average whole-rocks range between 5.98 and 0.49 wt. percent.

A magmatic origin is indicated for the type-2 LREE-enriched discordant dikes. On the basis of textural and field evidence, we suggest that the semiconcordant veins and discontinuous seams (type-1 LREE mineralization) may have formed in the presence of LREE-rich hydrothermal fluids. It is possible that both types of LREE mineralization may be penecontemporaneous, having formed in the marginal zone adjacent to a carbonate-rich magma that was highly charged with volatile constituents (for example, carbon dioxide, fluorine, and phosphorus) and strongly enriched in Ba, Sr, and LREE.

Both types of LREE-enriched rocks are comparable in grade to the world-class Bayan Obo (China) and Mountain Pass, Calif. (United States) deposits, which are also enriched in LREE. On the basis of several assumptions and employing a simple geometry for the zone of LREE enrichment, we estimate that at least 1 million metric tonnes (Mt) of LREE may be present in the Khanneshin Area of Interest. This comports well with the probabilistic estimate of 1.4 Mt of undiscovered REE resources in all of south Afghanistan (Peters and others, 2007). In addition to LREE, the Khanneshin carbonatite is also enriched in barium (>10 wt. percent), strontium (>6 wt. percent), phosphorus (~2 wt. percent), and uranium (>0.05 wt. percent).

1.0   Introduction

There is increased concern about the future availability of rare earth elements (REE) because of China's dominance as the supplier of more than 95 percent of world REE output, their decision to restrict exports of rare earth products, and the rapid increase in world-wide consumption of rare earth product. As a result, countries such as the United States, Japan, and member nations of the European Union face a future of tight supplies and high prices for rare earth products unless other sources of REE are found and developed (Long and others, 2010; U.S. Geological Survey, 2011, p. 128–129, 184–185). We report and describe a significant new deposit of light rare earth elements (LREE), estimated at 1 Mt, within the Khanneshin carbonatite complex of south Afghanistan. The potential resource is located in a remote and rugged part of the igneous complex in a region previously identified by Soviet geologists in the 1970s. This report reviews the geologic setting of LREE deposit, presents new geochemical data documenting the grade of LREE mineralization, briefly describes the mineralogy and mineralogical associations of the deposit, and presents a preliminary estimate of LREE resources based on our current understanding of the geology.

2.0   Geology of the Khanneshin Carbonatite Complex

2.1   Geologic Setting

The Khanneshin carbonatite is a deeply dissected alkaline igneous complex of Quaternary age that rises approximately 700 m above the Neogene sedimentary rocks of the Sistan basin, Helmand

Province, Afghanistan (fig. 1A). The carbonatite is one of eight proposed centers of alkaline igneous activity in southern Afghanistan (fig. 1B); all of these igneous centers except the Khanneshin complex are buried under Holocene-age sand and gravel of the Registan desert. These complexes, all of Neogene and younger age, are situated within the accreted terranes of the Helmand block south of the Har-i Rod fault. The terranes were accreted to south Asia in Mesozoic and younger time, but they are presently undergoing southwestward translation, and locally internal dilation, in response to continued northward thrusting of the Indian Plate (Krumsiek, 1980). Soviet geologists recognized the existence of both north-northeast- and west-northwest-striking regional faults in the Sistan basin, and they suggested that the Khanneshin carbonatite is distinctly linked to the crossing node of these faults in a region of relative dilation (Yeremenko, 1975; Cheremitsyn and Yeremenko, 1976; Alkhazov and others, 1978).

2.2 Geology

The igneous complex is broadly divisible into four parts (figs. 2 and 3): (1) a central vent, approximately 4 km in diameter; (2) a thin marginal zone (<1 km wide) of alkali metasomatized and outwardly dipping (5°–45°) Neogene sedimentary strata that form the basement rocks to the igneous complex; (3) a peripheral apron of volcanic and volcaniclastic strata extending another 3–5 km away from the central vent; and (4) small satellitic intrusions of sub-volcanic origin, no larger than 400 m in diameter, that crop out on the southern and southeastern periphery of the central intrusive massif

2.2.1 Rocks of the Central Vent

The igneous rocks of the central vent consist exclusively of holocrystalline, indurated carbonatite that forms the major topographic massif of the complex. The rocks of the central vent consist of medium- and coarse-grained carbonatite (sövite, Q_{isf}), confined to a stock approximately 2–3 km in diameter in the core of the massif, as well as fine- to medium-grained ankerite-barite alvikite (Q_{esf}) that forms a near continuous ring, 0.8–1.5 km wide, surrounding the central stock of sövite. At the margin of the central vent, where the intrusive rocks are in contact with Neogene sedimentary rocks, the Neogene strata are strongly altered, brecciated, and dike invaded, forming an outwardly dipping sequence of discolored and metasomatized albite- and calcite-rich fenites (fig. 2, N_a ; fig, 4A).

The sövites of the central stock are light-gray to reddish brown, spotted rocks, composed of calcite (70–95 percent) biotite (2–10 percent) strongly pleochroic amphibole (0–7 percent), acmite (0–5 percent), barite (0–4 percent), magnetite (0–5 percent), and apatite (0–4 percent). Important accessory minerals include zircon and pyrochlore.

In addition to sövite, the peripheral ring of the central vent is composed of black to dark gray, very dense, medium- to fine-grained carbonatite (alvikite, fig. 2, Q_{isf}). These alvikites are composed primarily of ankerite, dolomite, barite, and strontianite. The alvikites are described as agglomeratic (for example, Yeremenko, 1975; Cheremitsyn and Yeremenko, 1976; Alkhazov and others, 1978) because they contain abundant xenoliths of altered, mica-rich xenoliths (fenites, glimmerites, and camoforites) as well as blocks of coarse-grained sövite of the central massif (fig. 4A,D). They may also be fluidally banded, owing to the low viscosity of the CO_2-charged magma, and thus they locally have the appearance of layered volcanic rocks (that is, lava flows). Although some of the alvikites may be of extrusive volcanic origin, most of them are holocrystalline and fine-grained, with abundant fenitized xenoliths. We interpret them, therefore, to be of intrusive igneous origin. The alvikites consist mostly of calcite (10–15 percent), ankerite (5–50 percent), and dolomite (5–25 percent); however, an unusual variety of alvikite, very enriched in barium and strontium, crops out in the northeast part of the marginal zone. In these rocks, strontianite (5–20 percent), barite (5–50 percent), yellow-weathering REE-carbonate minerals, and celestine (0–10 percent) are common. Important accessory minerals in all varieties of alvikite are magnetite, phlogopite, galena, and hydrated iron oxides.

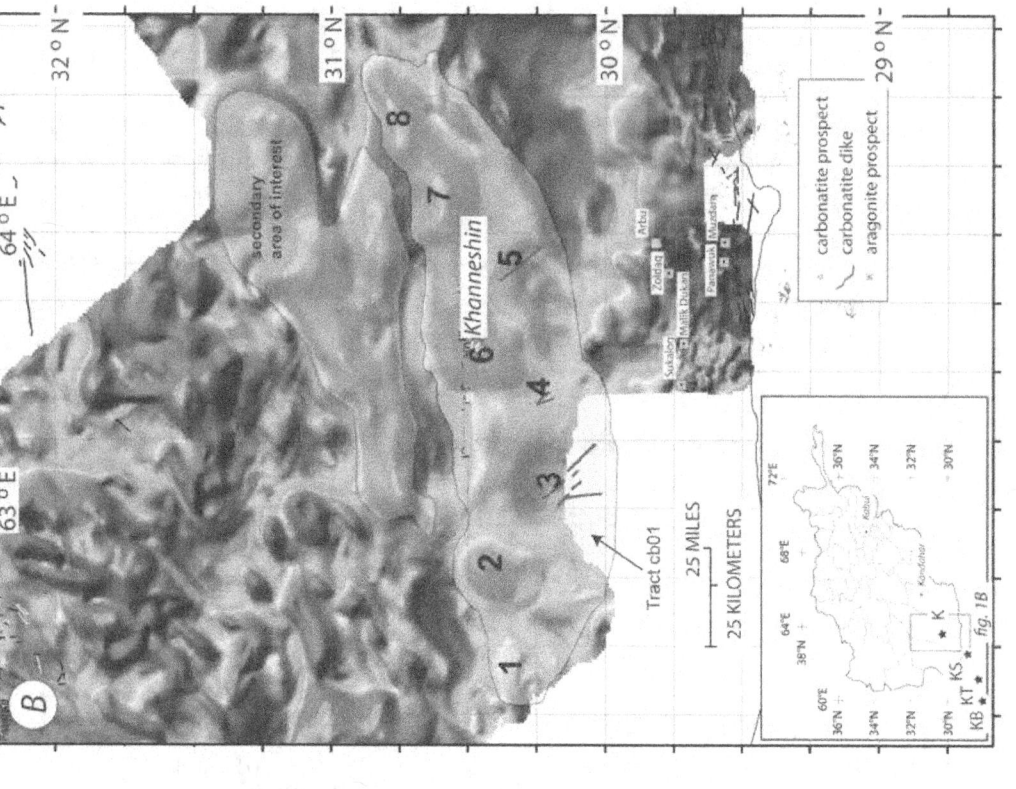

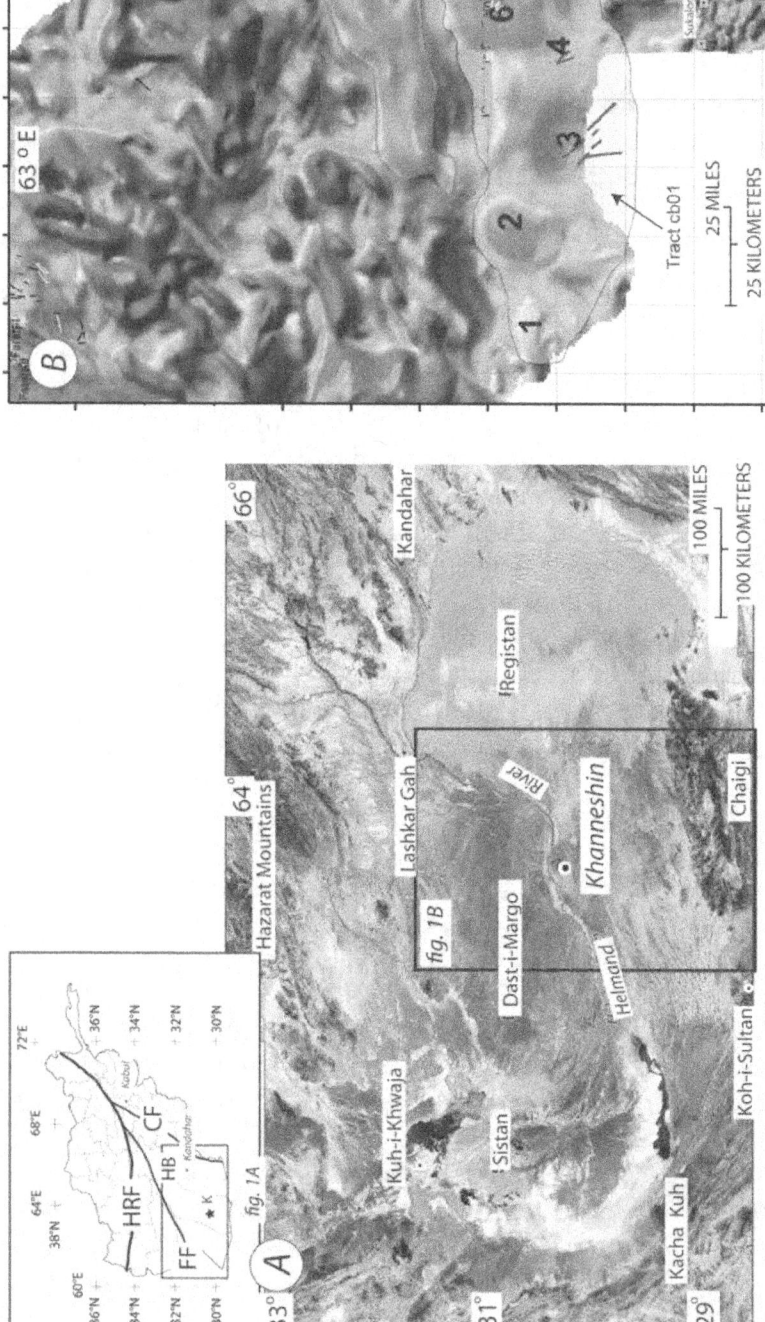

Figure 1. A, LANDSAT image of southern Afghanistan showing the location of the Khanneshin carbonatite complex within the Sistan basin. Inset map indicates the Har-i Rod fault (HRF), Chaman fault (CF), Farah fault (FF), the accreted terranes of the Helmand block (HB), and the Khanneshin carbonatite complex (K). Location of figure 1A shown by the black rectangle. B, Aeromagnetic map of south Afghanistan (Sweeney and others, 2006) showing the permissive tract of uranium-phosphorus-rare earth element (U-P-REE) mineralization (cb01) in the Helmand Basin. Numbers one through eight (1–8) refer to possible carbonatite centers within the tract based on the aeromagnetic data. These centers formed the basis of the quantitative estimate in Peters and others (2007). The single exposure of carbonatite is the Khanneshin complex of this report. Shown in B are the volcanoes of Quaternary age discussed in the text: KB (Koh-i Bazman), KT (Koh-i Taftan), KS (Koh-i Sultan), and K (Khanneshin).

4

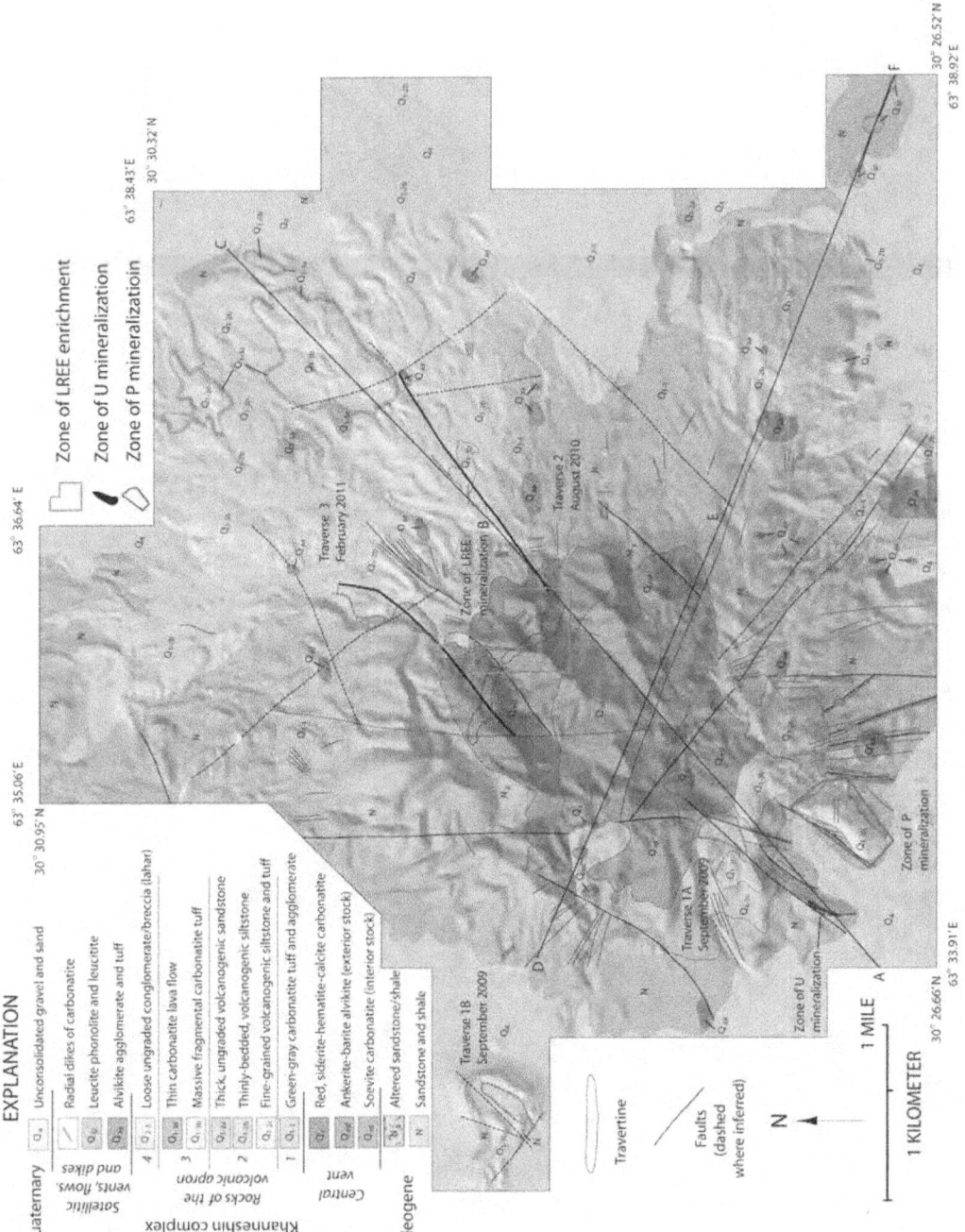

Figure 2. Geologic map of the Khanneshin carbonatite complex, Afghanistan, after Cheremitsyn and Yeremenko (1976), showing its principal bedrock divisions: (1) Neogene sedimentary strata, partly metasomatized, that form an upturned section of outwardly dipping strata away from the central intrusive vent. (2) The central intrusive vent (or massif) composed of sövite and medium- to fine-grained alvikite. The zone of light rare earth element (LREE) enrichment is located in the northeast part of the central vent (green box). (3) The apron of volcanic and volcano-sedimentary strata extending 5 km beyond from the central vent. (4) Small satellitic intrusive rocks and volcanic plugs, mostly on the southern peripheral margin of the complex, include alvikite agglomerate and leucite phonolite. The three traverses, 1 (A and B), 2, and 3, as well as the regions of rare earth element (REE), uranium (U), and phosphorus (P) enrichment, are indicted by labels.

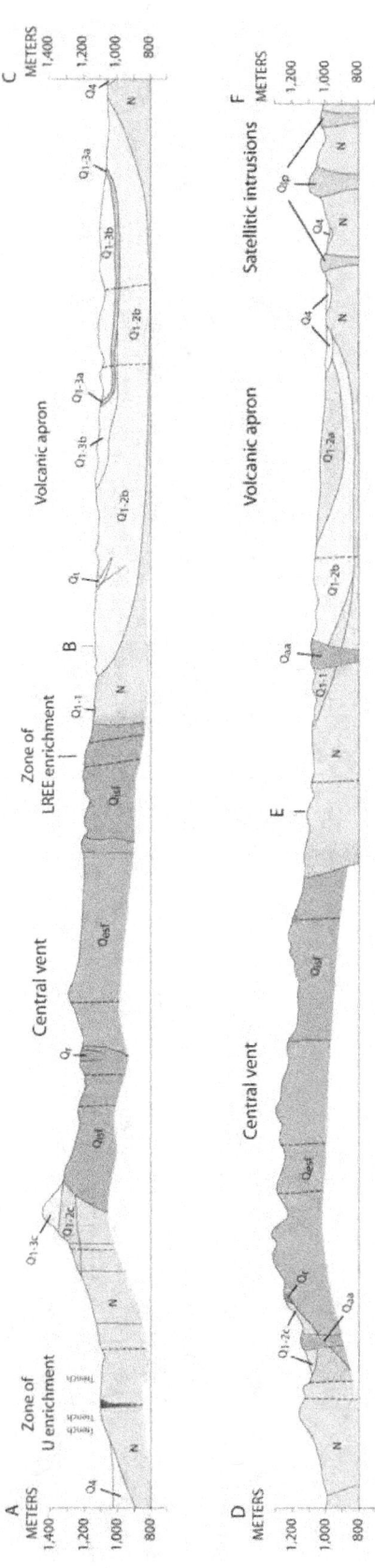

Figure 3. Two cross-sections through the Khanneshin carbonatite complex, Afghanistan, after Cheremitsyn and Yeremenko (1976), shown in figure 2: Line A-B-C, a northeast-southwest line of section through the zone of light rare earth element (LREE) enrichment and the zone of uranium (U) mineralization. Line D-E-F, a northwest-southeast line of section through the intrusive central vent and the plugs of leucite phonolite.

6

Figure 4. Field photographs showing the key rock types and relationships within the intrusive central vent and volcanic apron of the Khanneshin carbonatite complex, Afghanistan. *A,* Northwest view from the zone of rare earth element (REE) enrichment showing the Neogene strata (background) dipping modestly north and away from the intrusive rocks of the central vent (foreground). Vertical relief is approximately 150 m (note person for scale). *B,* Unconformable relationship between LREE-enriched alvikite (above) and typical alvikite of the marginal zone, intrusive central vent. Note that the underlying alvikite was cooled and intruded by a carbonatite dike before emplacement of the overlying LREE-enriched alvikite. *C,* Fine-grained alvikite at the margin of the central vent contains abundant xenoliths of fenitized country rock ("glimmerite") and sövite. *D,* Alvikite of the central vent, here also with xenoliths, is intruded by fine-grained dikes of carbonatite (compare with fig. 4b). *E,* Relationships observed in traverse 1B (fig. 2). View of the volcanic rocks (1 in circle) of the western apron (Q$_{1-3b}$) showing their relationship to older Neogene strata (2 in circle, N) and younger Quaternary gravels (3 in circle, Q$_4$).

The barium- and strontium-enriched alvikites (Q$_{esf}$) are located within a part of the vent that is bounded by north-northeast-trending faults with apparent normal displacement (fig. 2). It is best interpreted as a down-dropped block (graben) in which volcanic strata of the upper rim are juxtaposed against the intrusive rocks of the central vent without an intervening section of Neogene sedimentary strata. In contrast, rocks northwest and southeast of the block are strongly fenitized Neogene strata. It is conceivable, therefore, that the low-viscosity fluids or magma with extreme enrichments in Ba, Sr, and REE were focused by regional structures into this part of the central vent.

2.2.2   Volcanic and Volcano-Sedimentary Rocks

Pyroclastic and volcano-sedimentary rocks form an apron of stratified rocks that extends as much as 5 km beyond the central vent. The volcanic apron is best developed on the northeast and southeast margin of the carbonatite complex, but the apron is rather poorly developed on the western margin. Geologic mapping of the volcanic strata identified at least four volcano-sedimentary formations (fig. 2; Cheremitsyn and Yeremenko, 1976), each interpreted to correspond to a discrete eruptive and sedimentary stage. None of the volcanic formations has been studied in a modern-day petrologic sense, and their linkage to any plutonic part of the central vent is tentative at best. What is clear, however, is that the vast majority of the volcanic emissions are composed of some variety of carbonatite. The only known silicate-rich igneous rocks are three small plugs and lava flows of leucite phonolite in the southeastern part of the volcanic apron.

Part of the volcanic deposits near the central vent are composed of stratified dark red rocks that vary from very fine-grained tuff, some of them finely porphyritic, to sandstone-like rocks (fig. 2, Q_{1-2c}). Many of the fine grained rocks are composed of ferruginous carbonate that may represent volcanic emissions of thin carbonate ash. In addition to thin ferruginous carbonatite, the more coarse-grained rocks contain lithoclasts of ankeritic sövite and detrital quartz, plagioclase, and potassium feldspar. The amount of detrital material varies greatly, and ranges from as much as 10 to 70 modal percent. These rocks are best described as volcano-sedimentary tuffites, because of their high degree of sedimentary rounding and sorting.

The higher part of the volcanic section consists of bright orange-red rocks characterized by markedly higher iron content and, on the whole, a finer grain size (fig. 2, Q_{1-2b}). They are also highly sorted and occasionally cross bedded, indicating they are likely reworked and redeposited sediments of a primary volcanic source.

In the northern part of the volcanic field (fig. 2, Q_{1-1}), a mantle-like apron of coarse-grained agglomerate is mapped. The blocks are primarily sövite and ankerite-barite alvikite that range in size from a few centimeters to several meters in diameter. These blocks are cemented with very fine-grained greenish-brown carbonate. In some localities, signs of stratification are found amongst the blocks which are crudely stratified to form a macroscopic layering. The predominance of ankerite-barite carbonatite (alvikite) within the fragments suggests this unit formed as explosive eruption of ankerite-barite carbonatite.

Apparently linked to this eruption are coarsely laminated lithic tuffs on the western flank of the near-vent area (fig. 4E; fig. 2, Q_{1-3b}). Their lithic fragments include biotite sövite (similar to rocks of the central vent), barite carbonatite, magnetite-apatite alvikite, and phlogopitic "glimmerites." Unconformably overlying the laminated lithic tuffs are brick-red carbonatite tuffites. The southeastern part of the volcanic apron consists of green carbonatite tuffs, which form lenticular laminations overlying the brick-red tuffites. These are crystallo-lithoclastic, poorly cemented tuffs with fragments of ankerite sövite (30–70 percent), calcite (5–10 percent), phlogopite (2–8 percent), apatite (2–3 percent), potassium feldspar, and plagioclase.

The rock types described above constitute the near-vent rocks of the volcanic apron. In the distal parts of the apron, to the north and southeast, the volcanic strata are thin and strongly reworked by fluvial processes; they are best described as tuffaceous sedimentary deposits.

2.2.3 Satellitic Vents, Dikes, and Minor Intrusive Rocks

Five large plugs and several small extrusive masses of coarse-grained carbonatite crop out in the south, southeast, and west part of the Khanneshin carbonatite complex (fig. 2, Q_{aa}). These plugs and small extrusive masses are heterogeneous in composition and texture, but, in general, they are all holocrystalline igneous rocks consisting mostly of banded and spotted biotite-calcite sövite. The largest of the intrusive plugs consists of medium-grained alvikite with coarse- and very coarse-grained xenoliths of sövite, biotite-rich "glimmerites" (mica-rich inclusions) and potassium feldspar-rich country rock (fenites). In contrast, many of the smaller satellitic vents are dominated by medium-grained alvikite. In some of these plugs, very large (>1 m diameter) inclusions of coarse-grained sövite and "glimmerite" are abundant and large, and some outcrops have the appearance of giant intrusive breccias.

Three small plugs of leucitite and leucite phonolite also crop out in the southeast part of the volcanic apron (fig. 2, Q_{lp}). These are the only bodies of silicate rock in the Khanneshin complex. The leucite phonolites are dense, massive green-grey rocks with a thinly banded, finely spotted structure and porphyritic texture. Locally, they exhibit a spheroidal parting. The phenocrysts (50–70 percent) consist of leucite crystals 0.2–0.5 mm in diameter. The groundmass consists of sanidine, fine acicular aegerine aggregates, and minute crystals of nepheline, leucite, and carbonate.

Two groups of carbonatite dikes can be distinguished: (1) those composed of massive alvikite, ankerite-barite carbonatite, tuff-breccias of alvikite and (2) those composed of porous fine-grained carbonatite. The last type of dike is one of the youngest generations of igneous rocks in the complex. These dikes are composed of rhombic calcite phenocrysts in a fine-grained calcite matrix with very small crystals of disseminated magnetite, apatite, and rare aegerine and chlorite.

2.3 History of Igneous Activity

According to Cheremitsyn and Yeremenko (1976) and Vikhter and others (1976, 1978), igneous activity began with explosive eruption of ankerite alvikite from the central vent at Khanneshin carbonatite complex. This event was followed by forceful emplacement of coarse-grained sövite into the same vent. The presence of strongly metasomatized "glimmerites" and fenites within the central vent suggests the activity of fluorine-, sulfate- and phosphate-enriched fluids at depth. This initial phase was completed by the emplacement of REE enriched ankerite-barite carbonatite of the peripheral vent.

The succeeding phases commenced as an explosive eruption of common alvikite of the satellitic extrusive stocks and vents. These include various lava flows, volcanic tuffs, and volcanogenic sedimentary rocks of the volcanic apron. Emplaced into all of these are fine-grained carbonatites of the radial dykes. The final phase of activity was the eruption and emplacement of critically undersaturated silicate magma. These are represented by lava flows of leucite phonolite and intrusive brecciated plugs of leucitite in the southeastern part of the complex (figs. 2 and 3).

The Khanneshin complex was considered Pliocene to early Quaternary in age (Vikhter and others, 1978) because of the eroded appearance of the young, central vent, and the unpublished isotopic ages of between 1.4 and 2.8 to 5.0 million years reported by Abdullah and others (1977). However, Whitney (2006) cites an unpublished K-Ar age of 0.61 ± 0.05 million years (Richard Marvin, USGS, written commun. to Whitney), obtained on leucite from a plug of phonolite in the southeastern part of the complex. These phonolites are the youngest igneous rocks of the Khanneshin complex. Thus, we assign an early Quaternary age for the entire igneous complex, which is consistent with the unpublished K-Ar age, the fact that the central vent intrudes the Sistan beds of late Miocene age (Whitney, 2006), and the youngest volcanic strata are overlain by unconsolidated deposits of middle-upper Quaternary age (fig. 2, Q_4).

2.4 Metallogeny

The main nonfuel resources related to alkaline igneous rocks include barite, fluorspar, nepheline, REE, phosphate niobium, tantalum, zirconium, copper, uranium, and thorium. The Khanneshin carbonatite is the area of interest for three prospective nonfuel resources—REE, uranium (U) and phosphorus (P)—first identified and delineated by Soviet geologists in the 1970s (Chmyrev, 1976; Vikhter and others, 1976, 1978). Rare-earth element mineralization occurs mostly within the northeast marginal zone of the central vent, outlined in green in figure 2. Modestly high uranium and thorium concentrations (>200 parts per million, ppm) are reported in many rocks throughout the complex, but the greatest uranium concentrations are confined to silicified zones in the Neogene strata about 750 m southwest of the central vent. Finally, phosphorus is present in significant amounts, principally as apatite in rudaceous agglomerate, fenite xenoliths, and alvikite (fig. 2, Q_{1-3b}). Other commodities may be present in significant, but as yet undetermined, amounts; these include barite, fluorite, nepheline, niobium, tantalum, zirconium, and copper. In addition to the Khanneshin carbonatite, alkali syenite intrusive igneous rocks, consisting of volcanoes and intrusive plugs and dikes, are identified in south Afghanistan (Abdullah and others, 1977; Vikhter and others, 1976, 1978). On the basis of regional geologic considerations and Monte Carlo calculations, the USGS estimates that there is a 50-percent chance of one or more undiscovered deposits of REE and niobium in south Afghanistan. The mean estimated tonnage of these undiscovered resources is 1.4 Mt of REE and 3.5 Mt of niobium (Peters and others, 2007).

3.0   The Zone of LREE Enrichment

A high content of LREE is characteristic of the sövitic rocks, as well as of the barium- and strontium-rich rocks of the ankerite-barite alvikites. In the 1970s, Soviet geologists identified a polygonal area, underlain by rocks having extreme REE enrichment, in the northeast margin of the central vent (fig. 2, Q_{esf}). Within this area, outlined in green, several discordant dikes that are particularly rich in fluorite and LREE-carbonate minerals were identified. These dikes are tens of meters wide and as much as hundreds of meters long, and they contain as much as several wt. percent LREE.

Three 1-day scoping missions were completed by a team of USGS scientists and U.S. Department of Defense Task Force for Business and Stability Operations (TFBSO) personnel to the Khanneshin complex. Traverse 1, consisting of two different legs (1A and 1B) and completed in September 2009, examined the volcanic rocks in the southwestern part of the complex. In 2010 and 2011, two missions were made to the zone of LREE enrichment (fig. 2). Traverse 2, completed in August 2010 with 6 hours of allowed field time, intersected the southern boundary of LREE zone of enrichment and transected the contact between metasomatized Neogene strata and rocks of the central intrusive vent. Traverse 3, completed in February 2011, traversed the northern apron of volcanic strata and intersected the northwestern corner of the zone of LREE enrichment. Because of security concerns in this rugged part of the complex, the USGS-TFBSO field team was allowed less than two hours to complete traverse 3. Over the course of both missions, the field teams collected more than 50 rock samples representing the principal rocks of the mineralized zone; these were submitted for major-, trace, and rare earth element whole-rock geochemical analysis (tables 1–3). Polished thin-sections were made for each of the rock samples, and scanning-electron microscopy was conducted on a subset of these thin-sections.

Table 1. Whole-rock major-, trace-, and rare earth element (REE) concentration data, traverses 1A and 1B, Khanneshin carbonatite complex, Afghanistan.

[wt. %, weight percent; ppm, parts per million]

Unit	Description	Northing	Easting	Major elements										
				SiO2 wt. %	Al2O3 wt. %	Fe2O3(t) wt. %	MgO wt. %	CaO wt. %	Na2O wt. %	K2O wt. %	TiO2 wt. %	P2O5 wt. %	MnO wt. %	LOI wt. %
KH09002R	volcanic tuff	30.45918	63.57663	2.63	0.41	2.72	0.83	45.30	0.16	0.40	0.10	0.72	1.20	35.6
KH09003R	carbonatite dike	30.45901	63.57749	3.40	1.05	1.83	1.25	47.90	0.36	0.43	0.03	1.69	0.90	34.4
KH09004RP	alvikite agglomerate	30.45939	63.57956	14.30	3.02	7.98	2.19	35.80	0.37	2.61	0.20	1.97	0.33	27.7
KH09005R	alvikite agglomerate	30.45890	63.57753	17.60	3.79	9.42	2.66	34.90	0.74	2.06	0.21	2.32	0.33	23.4
KH09006R	alvikite agglomerate	30.45997	63.57998	14.30	2.42	8.43	2.81	36.00	0.41	2.62	0.17	3.72	0.49	24.8
KH09007R	alvikite agglomerate	30.46043	63.57931	28.80	6.85	9.90	2.34	25.30	0.40	5.58	0.45	1.38	0.43	17.1
KH09008R	alvikite agglomerate	30.45936	63.57565	11.50	1.89	8.92	2.94	39.40	0.63	0.72	0.15	3.63	0.40	27.4
KH09010R	alvikite agglomerate	30.45918	63.57666	15.80	3.27	8.37	2.41	36.60	0.78	1.74	0.19	2.45	0.38	24.6
KH09011RP	alvikite agglomerate	30.48074	63.54637	22.30	5.58	11.40	4.46	34.90	0.26	1.94	0.44	3.56	0.28	12.5
KH09012R	alvikite agglomerate	30.48082	63.54713	22.30	5.61	11.50	4.40	34.40	0.43	1.80	0.45	3.48	0.28	13.6
KH09013R	alvikite agglomerate	30.48086	63.54830	34.90	8.35	17.40	0.90	23.10	0.78	6.17	0.64	1.64	0.31	3.58
KH09014R	sandstone	30.48079	63.54882	60.10	5.76	1.44	0.71	14.60	0.75	3.50	0.19	0.12	0.03	11.9
KH09101R	volcanic tuff	30.46076	63.58070	31.30	8.45	8.18	2.77	21.70	0.77	6.64	0.34	1.01	0.49	15.6
KH09104R	carbonatite dike	30.45922	63.57607	14.60	3.13	7.92	2.07	36.00	0.29	3.30	0.19	2.07	0.33	28.5
KH09105	volcanic tuff	30.48179	63.54846	34.80	5.79	6.52	3.42	21.00	0.50	5.55	0.29	1.51	0.17	18.8

Unit	Description	Northing	Easting	Trace elements													
				Sc ppm	Be ppm	V ppm	Co ppm	Zn ppm	Ga ppm	Ge ppm	As ppm	Rb ppm	Sr ppm	Y ppm	Zr ppm	Nb ppm	Mo ppm
KH09002R	volcanic tuff	30.45918	63.57663	<5	46	157	2.1	279	17	NA	NA	15.5	>10,000	162.0	13.1	165	NA
KH09003R	carbonatite dike	30.45901	63.57749	<5	16	147	2.5	201	10	NA	NA	20.2	7,140	81.8	39.2	64	NA
KH09004RP	alvikite agglomerate	30.45939	63.57956	<5	14	115	11.8	158	13	NA	NA	87.2	>10,000	223.0	296.0	37	NA
KH09005R	alvikite agglomerate	30.45890	63.57753	<5	18	152	14.8	241	14	NA	NA	62.0	>10,000	151.0	435.0	41	NA
KH09006R	alvikite agglomerate	30.45997	63.57998	6	57	264	12.6	481	12	NA	NA	70.1	>10,000	203.0	339.0	65	NA
KH09007R	alvikite agglomerate	30.46043	63.57931	6	29	407	10.7	182	15	NA	NA	99.0	2,750	226.0	756.0	120	NA
KH09008R	alvikite agglomerate	30.45936	63.57565	6	19	200	11.3	159	11	NA	NA	54.1	7,520	175.0	456.0	59	NA
KH09010R	alvikite agglomerate	30.45918	63.57666	<5	17	165	12.7	208	13	NA	NA	67.7	>10,000	163.0	606.0	51	NA
KH09011RP	alvikite agglomerate	30.48074	63.54637	13	15	199	26.1	141	16	NA	NA	111.0	8,360	118.0	809.0	40	NA
KH09012R	alvikite agglomerate	30.48082	63.54713	13	14	185	25.5	141	16	NA	NA	119.0	8,350	118.0	755.0	39	NA
KH09013R	alvikite agglomerate	30.48086	63.54830	9	7	469	5.2	66	19	NA	NA	145.0	2,630	731.0	2,790.0	31	NA
KH09014R	sandstone	30.48079	63.54882	<5	<5	41	4.0	20	5	NA	NA	86.0	1,160	8.0	183.0	5	NA
KH09101R	volcanic tuff	30.46076	63.58070	8	19	288	9.5	176	16	NA	NA	107.0	6,970	193.0	519.0	111	NA
KH09104R	carbonatite dike	30.45922	63.57607	<5	14	116	11.4	156	12	NA	NA	83.3	9,060	219.0	284.0	38	NA
KH09105	volcanic tuff	30.48179	63.54846	7	12	70	14.1	96	11	NA	NA	164.0	4,310	64.7	347.0	26	NA

11

Trace elements—Continued

Unit	Description	Northing	Easting	Ba ppm	Bi ppm	Lu ppm	Hf ppm	Ta ppm	W ppm	Tl ppm	Pb ppm	Th ppm	U ppm
KH09002R	volcanic tuff	30.45918	63.57663	>10,000	2.8	0.92	<1	2	30	9.2	626	100	9.87
KH09003R	carbonatite dike	30.45901	63.57749	>10,000	8.2	1.36	<1	0.7	22	2.5	837	24.9	7.52
KH09004RP	alvikite agglomerate	30.45939	63.57956	3,060	0.8	2.63	9	2.7	3	1.4	79	102	7.45
KH09005R	alvikite agglomerate	30.45890	63.57753	3,180	1.2	1.22	5	2.4	2	4.7	121	106	15.3
KH09006R	alvikite agglomerate	30.45997	63.57998	5,090	5.0	1.48	10	2.2	4	6.2	309	107	8.57
KH09007R	alvikite agglomerate	30.46043	63.57931	4,320	2.3	1.71	19	3.8	50	4	167	78.9	7.47
KH09008R	alvikite agglomerate	30.45936	63.57565	5,220	1.6	1.64	12	2.8	6	1.4	124	123	10.4
KH09010R	alvikite agglomerate	30.45918	63.57666	3,610	1.6	1.32	6	2.9	1	10.5	149	105	26.6
KH09011RP	alvikite agglomerate	30.48074	63.54637	2,880	0.6	0.95	17	1.9	6	1.8	68	59.6	14.7
KH09012R	alvikite agglomerate	30.48082	63.54713	2,720	0.4	0.96	16	1.9	5	1.9	57	59.9	14.8
KH09013R	alvikite agglomerate	30.48086	63.54830	760	0.2	7.94	49	7.8	<1	1.2	26	116	12.7
KH09014R	sandstone	30.48079	63.54882	345	0.1	0.26	3	<0.5	2	0.7	13	3.5	3.16
KH09101R	volcanic tuff	30.46076	63.58070	5,410	3.1	1.32	10	8.6	36	2.7	193	118	16.7
KH09104R	carbonatite dike	30.45922	63.57607	2,690	0.8	2.44	8	2.6	3	1.3	79	96.7	7.35
KH09105	volcanic tuff	30.48179	63.54846	1,610	0.4	0.57	8	1.3	2	1.4	42	34.9	5.37

REEs

Unit	Description	Northing	Easting	La ppm	Ce ppm	Pr ppm	Nd ppm	Sm ppm	Eu ppm	Gd ppm	Tb ppm	Dy ppm	Ho ppm	Er ppm	Tm ppm	Yb ppm
KH09002R	volcanic tuff	30.45918	63.57663	1700	2550	268	821	105	21.3	70.2	9.7	42.8	6.44	13.2	1.32	6.6
KH09003R	carbonatite dike	30.45901	63.57749	922	1400	135	412	48.9	8.82	26.3	3.43	14.8	2.71	7.6	1.15	8.6
KH09004RP	alvikite agglomerate	30.45939	63.57956	492	1040	119	450	82.2	18.9	64.6	8.98	45.2	8.63	22.4	3	17.5
KH09005R	alvikite agglomerate	30.45890	63.57753	491	964	119	442	80.1	18.1	60.9	7.94	36.4	6.01	13.6	1.52	8.2
KH09006R	alvikite agglomerate	30.45997	63.57998	430	1140	105	399	79.4	18.7	66.1	9.27	45.2	7.52	17.2	1.97	10.5
KH09007R	alvikite agglomerate	30.46043	63.57931	320	713	82.5	332	78.7	19.9	73.1	10.9	55.6	9.15	20.6	2.23	11.6
KH09008R	alvikite agglomerate	30.45936	63.57565	484	1140	116	441	83.6	19	64	8.81	41.2	6.86	16.7	2.05	11
KH09010R	alvikite agglomerate	30.45918	63.57666	544	1060	128	482	85.5	18.8	63.4	8.3	37.6	6.23	14.1	1.56	8.7
KH09011RP	alvikite agglomerate	30.48074	63.54637	352	701	87.1	335	61.2	13.4	47.7	6.16	28.1	4.58	10.2	1.13	6.1
KH09012R	alvikite agglomerate	30.48082	63.54713	351	690	86.8	335	62.3	13.4	47.9	6.31	28.3	4.55	10.2	1.14	6.1
KH09013R	alvikite agglomerate	30.48086	63.54830	156	451	83.6	458	176	50.8	198	31.8	172	30.5	73.8	9.39	52.5
KH09014R	sandstone	30.48079	63.54882	12.4	21.6	2.79	10.3	2	0.49	1.73	0.25	1.46	0.28	0.82	0.09	0.9
KH09101R	volcanic tuff	30.46076	63.58070	376	760	90.2	344	72.2	17.6	61.1	9.05	45.3	7.55	16.5	1.8	9
KH09104R	carbonatite dike	30.45922	63.57607	457	1050	113	428	78.9	17.6	60.8	8.3	42.6	8.2	21.9	2.99	17.4
KH09105	volcanic tuff	30.48179	63.54846	162	329	41	157	29.5	6.55	23.4	3.05	14.6	2.45	5.61	0.65	3.7

12

Table 2. Major-, trace-, and rare earth element (REE) concentration data, traverse 2, Khanneshin carbonatite complex, Afghanistan.
[%, percent; ppm, parts per million]

| Unit | Description | Northing | Easting | Major elements | | | | | | | | | | |
				SiO₂ %	Al₂O₃ %	Fe₂O₃(t) %	MgO %	CaO %	Na₂O %	K₂O %	TiO₂ %	P₂O₅ %	MnO %	LOI %
AC-10-KH-05	alvikite	30.46884	63.59335	NA	0.45	NA	NA	NA	NA	NA	NA	0.708	0.759	NA
RT-10K-03	fluorite-REE dike	30.47290	63.59799	NA	0.14	NA	NA	NA	NA	NA	0.003	0.082	>1.3	NA
RT-10K-13	alvikite	30.47363	63.60064	NA	3.98	NA	NA	NA	NA	NA	>0.17	0.914	>1.3	NA
AC-10-KH-01	alvikite	30.47013	63.59568	NA	0.30	NA	NA	NA	NA	NA	0.087	0.936	>1.3	NA
RT-10K-2B	carbonatite dike	30.47407	63.60501	NA	0.36	NA	NA	NA	NA	NA	0.028	0.165	1.252	NA
RT-10K-4B	carbonatite dike	30.47035	63.59533	NA	1.40	NA	NA	NA	NA	NA	0.065	1.14	0.684	NA
FH-10-KH-02	alvikite	30.46884	63.59355	NA	0.10	NA	NA	NA	NA	NA	0.009	>2.3	>1.3	NA
FH-10-KH-04	alvikite	30.47354	63.59877	NA	1.08	NA	NA	NA	NA	NA	0.036	1.346	0.969	NA
FH-10-KH-05	alvikite	30.46816	63.59297	NA	0.22	NA	NA	NA	NA	NA	0.024	0.099	0.307	NA
FH-10-KH-08	alvikite	30.46858	63.59299	NA	0.12	NA	NA	NA	NA	NA	0.008	0.366	>1.3	NA
AC-10-KH-04	alvikite	30.46884	63.59335	NA	5.85	NA	NA	NA	NA	NA	>0.17	1.17	1.209	NA
RT-10K-5A	sövite	30.46884	63.59361	NA	1.37	NA	NA	NA	NA	NA	0.068	0.481	0.547	NA
RT-10K-5B	alvikite	30.46884	63.59361	NA	0.09	NA	NA	NA	NA	NA	0.022	>2.3	>1.3	NA
RT-10K-5C	apatite alvikite	30.46884	63.59361	NA	0.17	NA	NA	NA	NA	NA	0.014	>2.3	>1.3	NA
RT-10K-5D	apatite alvikite	30.46884	63.59361	NA	0.13	NA	NA	NA	NA	NA	0.023	1.365	>1.3	NA
RT-10K-09	sövite	30.47087	63.59591	NA	1.25	NA	NA	NA	NA	NA	0.059	>2.3	0.931	NA
RT-10K-12	alvikite dike	30.47388	63.59966	NA	0.32	NA	NA	NA	NA	NA	0.024	1.678	1.015	NA
RT-10K-5E	alvikite tuff	30.46884	63.59361	NA	0.11	NA	NA	NA	NA	NA	0.015	1.721	>1.3	NA
FH-10-KH-03	alvikite	30.46726	63.59227	NA	>9.4	NA	NA	NA	NA	NA	>0.17	1.885	0.593	NA
FH-10-KH-06	alvikite	30.46806	63.59283	NA	>9.4	NA	NA	NA	NA	NA	>0.17	0.163	0.595	NA
FH-10-KH-07	alvikite	30.47056	63.59573	NA	1.28	NA	NA	NA	NA	NA	1.012	0.418	0.657	NA
RT-10K-6A	alvikite tuff	30.46719	63.59228	NA	3.59	NA	NA	NA	NA	NA	0.149	1.057	0.415	NA
RT-10K-6B	alvikite tuff	30.46719	63.59228	NA	3.63	NA	NA	NA	NA	NA	0.152	2.063	1.105	NA
RT-10K-6C	alvikite tuff	30.46719	63.59228	NA	0.15	NA	NA	NA	NA	NA	0.016	0.242	>1.3	NA
RT-10K-6D	alvikite tuff	30.46719	63.59228	NA	>9.4	NA	NA	NA	NA	NA	>0.17	0.437	0.535	NA
RT-10K-6E	alvikite tuff	30.46719	63.59228	NA	2.49	NA	NA	NA	NA	NA	0.096	0.391	0.16	NA
RT-10K-1A	alvikite agglomerate	30.47335	63.60572	NA	2.88	NA	NA	NA	NA	NA	0.142	0.777	>1.3	NA
RT-10K-07	alvikite	30.46859	63.59301	NA	0.24	NA	NA	NA	NA	NA	0.017	0.221	>1.3	NA
RT-10K-08	alvikite agglomerate	30.46975	63.59528	NA	7.69	NA	NA	NA	NA	NA	>0.17	1.285	0.597	NA
FH-10-KH-01	alvikite	30.47013	63.59568	NA	1.21	NA	NA	NA	NA	NA	0.125	0.802	0.506	NA
AC-10-KH-02	alvikite	30.47013	63.59568	NA	0.17	NA	NA	NA	NA	NA	0.014	0.95	0.306	NA
AC-10-KH-03	alvikite	30.46870	63.59371	NA	0.09	NA	NA	NA	NA	NA	0.008	>2.3	>1.3	NA
RT-10K-10	alvikite tuff	30.47191	63.59710	NA	0.46	NA	NA	NA	NA	NA	0.084	0.342	1.239	NA
RT-10K-11	alvikite tuff	30.47358	63.59824	NA	0.47	NA	NA	NA	NA	NA	0.119	1.642	>1.3	NA
AC-10-KH-06	alvikite	30.46872	63.59368	NA	0.09	NA	NA	NA	NA	NA	0.033	0.367	>1.3	NA
RT-10K-4A	alvikite tuff	30.47035	63.59533	NA	1.04	NA	NA	NA	NA	NA	0.095	0.099	1.284	NA
RT-10K-1B	alvikite tuff	30.47335	63.60572	NA	0.15	NA	NA	NA	NA	NA	0.041	1.468	>1.3	NA
RT-10K-2A	siltstone	30.47407	63.60501	NA	8.94	NA	NA	NA	NA	NA	>0.17	0.056	0.227	NA
FH-10-KH-10	alvikite	30.47385	63.60465	NA	>9.4	NA	NA	NA	NA	NA	>0.17	0.283	0.151	NA

13

Unit	Description	Northing	Easting	Trace elements											
				Sc ppm	Be ppm	V ppm	Co ppm	Zn ppm	Ga ppm	Ge ppm	As ppm	Rb ppm	Sr ppm	Y ppm	Zr ppm
AC-10-KH-05	alvikite	30.46884	63.59335	0.1	4	5,222	8.1	1,847	5.8	NA	58	5.5	4,538	5	32.3
RT-10K-03	fluorite-REE dike	30.47290	63.59799	0.6	4.7	47.3	1.9	177	49.8	NA	2,882	3.1	28,051	156	44.1
RT-10K-13	alvikite	30.47363	63.60064	8.2	35.8	193.9	8	622	19.5	NA	208	47.1	13,752	223	52
AC-10-KH-01	alvikite	30.47013	63.59568	7.6	44.4	166.8	2.1	952	41.4	NA	2,360	9.6	27,885	880	84.3
RT-10K-2B	carbonatite dike	30.47407	63.60501	11.2	16.8	122.8	5.8	439	14.8	NA	379	5.3	28,233	198	32.3
RT-10K-4B	carbonatite dike	30.47035	63.59533	<0.1	38.4	110.5	6	308	12.7	NA	228	18.7	11,270	172	48.5
FH-10-KH-02	alvikite	30.46884	63.59355	<0.1	14.2	35.4	0.5	951	58.3	NA	6,498	2.9	22,926	74	256.6
FH-10-KH-04	alvikite	30.47354	63.59877	3.4	5.7	80.9	2.9	195	10.5	NA	380	21.3	27,224	210	17.4
FH-10-KH-05	alvikite	30.46816	63.59297	1.2	12.4	39.1	1.8	>10,000	30.5	NA	1,012	3.2	14,720	37	64.2
FH-10-KH-08	alvikite	30.46858	63.59299	0.6	15.4	42.5	0.5	2,233	57.8	NA	3,816	2.7	25,693	46	58.8
AC-10-KH-04	alvikite	30.46884	63.59335	0.5	19.2	154.9	6.1	2,155	15.5	NA	118	121.2	19,828	33	55.8
RT-10K-5A	sövite	30.46884	63.59361	4.8	4.7	106.2	2.6	169	10.1	NA	148	34.2	15,417	43	30.7
RT-10K-5B	alvikite	30.46884	63.59361	<0.1	11.1	36.1	0.6	2,811	59.2	NA	<1.5	4.1	20,171	24	100.6
RT-10K-5C	apatite alvikite	30.46884	63.59361	<0.1	4.8	32.4	0.4	2,382	52.2	NA	>10,000	2.2	14,000	122	177
RT-10K-5D	apatite alvikite	30.46884	63.59361	<0.1	11.6	31	0.4	1,243	59.2	NA	<1.5	3.1	18,109	75	52.1
RT-10K-09	sövite	30.47087	63.59591	2.3	7.7	116.5	5	144	10.4	NA	99	31.5	13,851	202	345
RT-10K-12	alvikite dike	30.47388	63.59966	3.7	4	78.9	8.4	75	6.8	NA	159	5.5	18,695	306	17
RT-10K-5E	alvikite	30.46884	63.59361	<0.1	15.2	31.1	0.4	2,009	55.6	NA	>10,000	4.6	17,163	28	116.3
FH-10-KH-03	alvikite	30.46726	63.59227	3.2	4.4	250	16	507	16.5	NA	63	66.3	6,491	23	70.7
FH-10-KH-06	alvikite	30.46806	63.59283	7.1	7.1	208.8	14.7	239	11	NA	<1.5	32.7	2,331	16	19
FH-10-KH-07	alvikite	30.47056	63.59573	7.9	10.2	107.4	3.9	510	15.3	NA	255	33	15,124	286	68.7
RT-10K-6A	alvikite tuff	30.46719	63.59228	6.1	10.6	128	5.4	220	10.3	NA	157	51.4	5,441	40	260
RT-10K-6B	alvikite tuff	30.46719	63.59228	3.4	9.5	89.8	7.1	389	13.3	NA	107	76.4	12,116	111	209
RT-10K-6C	alvikite tuff	30.46719	63.59228	2.9	6.3	61	1.4	1,041	25.8	NA	562	7.8	22,706	127	46
RT-10K-6D	alvikite tuff	30.46719	63.59228	5.6	11.3	241.5	14.9	282	10.9	NA	<1.5	40.1	2,761	19	45
RT-10K-6E	alvikite tuff	30.46719	63.59228	1	4.6	85.7	3.2	116	4.1	NA	106	37.9	3,153	18	41
RT-10K-1A	alvikite agglomerate	30.47335	63.60572	10.8	14.7	172.3	6.1	364	18	NA	479	49.7	18,941	255	80.4
RT-10K-07	alvikite	30.46859	63.59301	0.9	19.2	55	1.3	3,347	32.4	NA	1,107	4.4	40,469	54	34
RT-10K-08	alvikite agglomerate	30.46975	63.59528	4.9	10.3	114	10.1	268	13.9	NA	86	60.5	10,909	83	615
FH-10-KH-01	alvikite	30.47013	63.59568	0.9	5.8	59.9	4.3	383	14.5	NA	204	42.3	16,425	61	11.1
AC-10-KH-02	alvikite	30.47013	63.59568	0.8	2.1	38.8	1.1	33	9.8	NA	104	5.6	23,451	80	8.4
AC-10-KH-03	alvikite	30.46870	63.59371	<0.1	4.9	31.2	1.1	793	13.9	NA	316	4.9	20,751	97	69
RT-10K-10	alvikite tuff	30.47191	63.59710	2.9	3.1	288.8	5.5	969	22.3	NA	407	37.7	26,676	174	42
RT-10K-11	alvikite tuff	30.47358	63.59824	4.6	4.5	275	3.9	351	18.1	NA	323	4.2	17,623	301	81
AC-10-KH-06	alvikite	30.46872	63.59368	1.1	11.5	94.5	1.1	1,240	17.8	NA	509	2.7	31,607	145	29.3
RT-10K-4A	alvikite tuff	30.47035	63.59533	3.5	5.2	108.5	3.5	1,815	25.5	NA	566	26.4	20,739	416	22.7
RT-10K-1B	alvikite tuff	30.47335	63.60572	3.4	66.3	84.8	4.2	88	30.9	NA	907	1.8	33,723	572	222.5
RT-10K-2A	siltstone	30.47407	63.60501	16.7	63.4	259.1	7.9	114	9.3	NA	<1.5	47.3	653	62	145.3
FH-10-KH-10	alvikite	30.47385	63.60465	22.6	>100	246.1	12.9	116	13.3	NA	118	40.6	1,145	111	114.5

14

Unit	Description	Northing	Easting	Trace elements—Continued											
				Nb ppm	Mo ppm	Ba ppm	Bi ppm	Lu ppm	Hf ppm	Ta ppm	W ppm	Tl ppm	Pb ppm	Th ppm	U ppm
AC-10-KH-05	alvikite	30.46884	63.59335	429.6	3.5	1,420	10.6	0.1	0.7	10.5	NA	4.6	1,100	8.1	33.1
RT-10K-03	fluorite-REE dike	30.47290	63.59799	5.5	10.4	4,651	0.3	0.7	1.6	2.1	NA	1.4	93	50.4	29.1
RT-10K-13	alvikite	30.47363	63.60064	295	6.1	1,124	10.6	2.12	1.68	5.73	NA	2.2	848	279	74.7
AC-10-KH-01	alvikite	30.47013	63.59568	173	17.8	385	0.4	2.2	1.9	2	NA	6.6	562	465.5	27.8
RT-10K-2B	carbonatite dike	30.47407	63.60501	162.7	3.8	8,824	6.8	2	0.8	2	NA	15.9	631	340.5	20.8
RT-10K-4B	carbonatite dike	30.47035	63.59533	22.9	4.1	5,062	2.2	0.8	1.5	2.3	NA	1.3	229	90	44.4
FH-10-KH-02	alvikite	30.46884	63.59355	1.6	1.6	748	0	0.4	2.7	2.5	NA	0.9	352	52.1	24.1
FH-10-KH-04	alvikite	30.47354	63.59877	21	3	7,163	4.5	1.6	0.6	1.3	NA	2.4	235	113.6	17.5
FH-10-KH-05	alvikite	30.46816	63.59297	129.1	17.7	2,324	1	0.4	2.6	4	NA	2.5	6,560	35.1	67.8
FH-10-KH-08	alvikite	30.46858	63.59299	15.7	15.8	721	0	0.6	1.7	3.1	NA	0.5	342	52.8	24.2
AC-10-KH-04	alvikite	30.46884	63.59335	569	2.1	998	10.4	0.3	1.2	11.5	NA	13.6	827	22.1	412
RT-10K-5A	sövite	30.46884	63.59361	21.8	2.2	2,514	0.2	0.4	0.8	1.3	NA	3.1	41	9.3	8.2
RT-10K-5B	alvikite	30.46884	63.59361	58.3	21.8	674	0	0.3	1.8	2.8	NA	2.2	1,483	54.9	60.5
RT-10K-5C	apatite alvikite	30.46884	63.59361	9.6	2.6	1,365	0	0.4	2	2	NA	0.5	469	50.3	48.8
RT-10K-5D	apatite alvikite	30.46884	63.59361	218.5	6.5	1,164	0	0.3	1.6	2.6	NA	1.3	1,476	25.2	79.8
RT-10K-09	sövite	30.47087	63.59591	30	2.9	2,840	0.2	1.34	2.99	2.16	NA	2	86	82.1	12.1
RT-10K-12	alvikite dike	30.47388	63.59966	80	21.5	7,048	15.1	1.95	0.85	0.58	NA	4.5	675	346.5	24.5
RT-10K-5E	alvikite	30.46884	63.59361	27.1	4.3	576	0	0.3	2.2	2.6	NA	1.9	1,042	75.5	32.6
FH-10-KH-03	alvikite	30.46726	63.59227	86.7	0.3	1,618	14.2	0.2	1.4	7.1	NA	2	153	10.9	12.9
FH-10-KH-06	alvikite	30.46806	63.59283	47.5	0.5	7,940	3.1	0.1	0.8	1.3	NA	3.3	133	32	3.6
FH-10-KH-07	alvikite	30.47056	63.59573	271	6.7	141	20.9	0.9	2.3	18.2	NA	3	1,463	126.2	107.5
RT-10K-6A	alvikite tuff	30.46719	63.59228	55	0.6	2,323	20	0.45	4.23	6.71	NA	4.6	630	21.5	12.2
RT-10K-6B	alvikite tuff	30.46719	63.59228	57	1.1	3,244	4.4	0.82	4.22	4.66	NA	4.4	835	128	15.1
RT-10K-6C	alvikite tuff	30.46719	63.59228	140	4.4	488	4.1	0.67	1.27	0.91	NA	4.2	1,020	222.5	28.6
RT-10K-6D	alvikite tuff	30.46719	63.59228	84	0.5	7,428	1.5	0.16	1.24	7.96	NA	3.5	98	8.3	4.1
RT-10K-6E	alvikite tuff	30.46719	63.59228	31	1.4	66	2.2	0.15	1.21	1.45	NA	1.6	162	10.9	4.5
RT-10K-1A	alvikite agglomerate	30.47335	63.60572	110	2	1,553	19.2	1.3	1.9	4.2	NA	15	1,160	478.9	52.2
RT-10K-07	alvikite	30.46859	63.59301	50	53.5	527	0.4	0.56	1.94	2.22	NA	3.9	1,230	49.8	32
RT-10K-08	alvikite agglomerate	30.46975	63.59528	84	0.8	8,751	3.4	0.65	9.38	4.66	NA	4.7	314	62.3	14.8
FH-10-KH-01	alvikite	30.47013	63.59568	33.5	9.6	1,812	35.9	0.5	0.5	1.6	NA	2.4	1,210	15.1	3.2
AC-10-KH-02	alvikite	30.47013	63.59568	6.6	0.5	1,374	8.6	0.7	0.3	0.5	NA	0.5	334	45.8	3.5
AC-10-KH-03	alvikite	30.46870	63.59371	15.7	6.2	735	7.4	0.6	1.2	1	NA	2	652	69	45.4
RT-10K-10	alvikite tuff	30.47191	63.59710	362	3.3	6,631	6.5	0.73	1.52	15.07	NA	7.7	1,301	45.4	54.6
RT-10K-11	alvikite tuff	30.47358	63.59824	362	5.2	5,314	21.5	1.3	3.04	7.15	NA	8.2	2,174	233.9	311
AC-10-KH-06	alvikite	30.46872	63.59368	44.7	9.5	1,110	6.9	0.7	0.8	2.7	NA	10.8	829	218.7	21.4
RT-10K-4A	alvikite tuff	30.47035	63.59533	232	22.2	7,320	13.4	1.1	1.1	12.2	NA	39.5	1,848	80.2	74.3
RT-10K-1B	alvikite tuff	30.47335	63.60572	56.4	8.8	749	17	2.2	2.7	2.1	NA	0.5	1,288	364.7	80.7
RT-10K-2A	siltstone	30.47407	63.60501	205.1	0.8	684	0.2	0.8	4.2	0.7	NA	4.1	36	48	1.7
FH-10-KH-10	alvikite	30.47385	63.60465	186.8	1.3	318	0.5	1.4	3.9	1.2	NA	6	81	77.2	9.5

15

| | | | | REEs | | | | | | | | | | | | |
| Unit | Description | Northing | Easting | La | Ce | Pr | Nd | Sm | Eu | Gd | Tb | Dy | Ho | Er | Tm | Yb |
				ppm	ppm	ppm	ppm	ppm	ppm	ppm	ppm	ppm	ppm	ppm	ppm	ppm
AC-10-KH-05	alvikite	30.46884	63.59335	349	652	73	244	29.7	5.6	20.8	1.2	2.5	0.3	1.5	0.1	0.6
RT-10K-03	fluorite-REE dike	30.47290	63.59799	9,198	10,536	673.9	1,430	119	49.8	198	10.5	25.3	3.6	12.7	1	5
RT-10K-13	alvikite	30.47363	63.60064	1,625	3,183	321	1,148	153	37.95	131.8	11.88	45.18	6.18	17.66	2.07	14.02
AC-10-KH-01	alvikite	30.47013	63.59568	5,816	8,217	708.2	2,079	292	84.9	282	25.5	95.1	13.1	33.7	2.9	16.4
RT-10K-2B	carbonatite dike	30.47407	63.60501	1,422	2,262	212.8	624	72.3	19.3	89.2	9.7	40.9	5.9	15.7	1.8	12.8
RT-10K-4B	carbonatite dike	30.47035	63.59533	640	1,161	127.1	426	63.3	13.4	51.7	5.1	30.3	5.9	14.7	1.6	7.6
FH-10-KH-02	alvikite	30.46884	63.59355	5,927	11,095	954.2	2,581	240	69.2	236	12.2	18.3	2.2	12.5	0.5	3.1
FH-10-KH-04	alvikite	30.47354	63.59877	956	1,540	155.4	519	91.9	23.6	89.4	11.1	51.4	7.7	18.6	2.1	11.3
FH-10-KH-05	alvikite	30.46816	63.59297	7,556	6,545	366.1	691	43.8	34.1	92.7	3.8	8	1.3	5.3	0.5	2.7
FH-10-KH-08	alvikite	30.46858	63.59299	7,530	11,254	849.2	2,157	189.7	71.5	214	10.2	14.9	1.7	10.4	0.5	3.8
AC-10-KH-04	alvikite	30.46884	63.59335	340	590	59.5	191	25.9	5.8	23.2	2.2	8.3	1.3	3.6	0.4	1.9
RT-10K-5A	sövite	30.46884	63.59361	281	549	60.6	208	34.3	7.2	28.2	2.8	11	1.6	4.2	0.5	2.7
RT-10K-5B	alvikite	30.46884	63.59361	6,408	11,046	850.3	2,163	180	66.7	204	9.4	13.2	1.5	9.4	0.3	2.2
RT-10K-5C	apatite alvikite	30.46884	63.59361	4,783	9,505	860.7	2,543	257	68.7	231	12.9	23.4	2.5	12	0.5	3
RT-10K-5D	apatite alvikite	30.46884	63.59361	6,562	11,053	862.2	2,285	207	70.9	227	11	18.1	2	10.7	0.4	2.5
RT-10K-09	sövite	30.47087	63.59591	426	919	108	430	68	17.41	64.67	8.27	43.38	6.58	16.08	1.76	10.1
RT-10K-12	alvikite dike	30.47388	63.59966	458	986	117	473	88	25.33	95.78	14.03	73.82	10.77	24.41	2.68	14.15
RT-10K-5E	alvikite	30.46884	63.59361	6,094	10,609	841.4	2,220	179	63.7	207	9.3	12.8	1.4	9.4	0.3	2.3
FH-10-KH-03	alvikite	30.46726	63.59227	117	245	27.9	103	18.4	4.3	16.1	1.8	7.1	1	2.6	0.3	1.4
FH-10-KH-06	alvikite	30.46806	63.59283	117	192	20	68	11.8	4.5	11	1.1	4.6	0.7	1.6	0.2	1.1
FH-10-KH-07	alvikite	30.47056	63.59573	932	1,995	227.5	835	154.2	36.4	139	16.8	73.5	10.1	22.8	1.9	8.5
RT-10K-6A	alvikite tuff	30.46719	63.59228	169	335	37	139	20	5.07	18.32	2.02	8.86	1.33	3.61	0.45	3.01
RT-10K-6B	alvikite tuff	30.46719	63.59228	831	1,497	150	527	70	16.98	66.86	6.15	25.67	3.55	9.17	0.94	5.97
RT-10K-6C	alvikite tuff	30.46719	63.59228	1,784	4,071	458	1,617	151	34.25	127.9	8.23	23.17	3.16	10.92	0.76	5.19
RT-10K-6D	alvikite tuff	30.46719	63.59228	85	167	19	71	12	4.28	10.4	1.09	5.16	0.76	2.11	0.21	1.25
RT-10K-6E	alvikite tuff	30.46719	63.59228	65	142	17	70	12	2.84	9.62	1.01	4.79	0.71	1.75	0.18	1.15
RT-10K-1A	alvikite agglomerate	30.47335	63.60572	1,593	2,659	269.4	874	135	39.6	126	13	54.2	8	19.1	1.9	10.2
RT-10K-07	alvikite	30.46859	63.59301	7,838	7,101	441	1,048	83	6.71	113.1	5.13	12.55	1.7	6.71	0.62	4.37
RT-10K-08	alvikite agglomerate	30.46975	63.59528	554	1,011	110	412	57	14.1	50.29	4.89	20.49	2.94	7.56	0.74	4.5
FH-10-KH-01	alvikite	30.47013	63.59568	495	939	97.6	316	38.9	9	36.1	3.3	13.8	2.4	7	0.8	3.9
AC-10-KH-02	alvikite	30.47013	63.59568	722	1,372	148.3	494	62.6	13.1	54.5	5.1	19.9	2.9	8.7	0.9	5.3
AC-10-KH-03	alvikite	30.46870	63.59371	1,105	1,996	217.7	673	78.8	18.7	70.6	5.9	20.7	3.2	9.6	1	4.9
RT-10K-10	alvikite tuff	30.47191	63.59710	1,554	3,287	371	1,440	190	13.18	151.8	13.12	44.98	5.23	13.18	1.02	5.96
RT-10K-11	alvikite tuff	30.47358	63.59824	1,484	3,215	355	1,396	209	52.8	177.5	16.96	65.4	8.16	19.53	1.76	10.07
AC-10-KH-06	alvikite	30.46872	63.59368	2,245	3,210	298.2	874	111	30.7	112	9.7	31.9	4.2	11.2	1	5.7
RT-10K-4A	alvikite tuff	30.47035	63.59533	1,503	2,835	311.6	1,072	150	30.3	128	12.6	53	9.4	26.1	2.3	18.9
RT-10K-1B	alvikite tuff	30.47335	63.60572	2,535	5,124	533.4	1,842	268	56.5	234	24.1	92.9	12.7	32.5	3	16.5
RT-10K-2A	siltstone	30.47407	63.60501	38	65	7.4	27	8.2	2.6	10.8	1.9	11.7	2	5.5	0.8	5.3
FH-10-KH-10	alvikite	30.47385	63.60465	31	62	7.1	29	10.1	3.6	14.6	3	20.6	4	10.8	1.5	9.5

Table 3. Major- and trace-, and rare earth element (REE) concentration data, traverse 3, Khanneshin carbonatite complex, Afghanistan.
[wt. %, weight percent; ppm, parts per million]

Unit	Description	Northing	Easting	Major elements										
				SiO₂ wt. %	Al₂O₃ wt. %	Fe₂O₃(t) wt. %	MgO wt. %	CaO wt. %	Na₂O wt. %	K₂O wt. %	TiO₂ wt. %	P₂O₅ wt. %	MnO wt. %	LOI wt. %
RT-11K-1A1	Type-2 fluorine-rich dike	30.47976	63.59494	0.99	0.07	1.84	5.25	22.97	0.08	0.17	0.01	0.25	1.16	21.15
RT-11K-1A2	Type-2 fluorine-rich dike	30.47976	63.59494	0.82	0.06	1.70	4.56	21.68	0.07	0.15	0.01	0.25	0.90	20.17
RT-11K-1B2	Type-2 fluorine-rich dike	30.47976	63.59494	0.83	0.06	4.14	5.41	22.66	0.11	0.15	0.00	0.25	1.13	20.39
RT-11K-2A2	Type-1 concordantly banded REE vein	30.47924	63.59546	0.23	0.02	3.14	7.10	19.17	0.28	0.02	0.01	2.13	1.90	24.23
RT-11K-2B1	Type-1 concordantly banded REE vein	30.47924	63.59546	0.22	0.03	3.14	6.31	16.91	0.23	0.02	0.01	1.76	1.78	23.19
RT-11K-2B2	Type-1 concordantly banded REE vein	30.47924	63.59546	0.20	0.02	2.98	6.07	17.19	0.26	0.02	0.00	2.03	1.82	22.71
RT-11K-3B31	Type-2 patite-rich dike	30.47883	63.59459	1.00	0.23	3.81	3.30	16.90	0.16	0.23	0.02	1.41	1.97	20.34
RT-11K-3B32	Type-2 apatite-rich dike	30.47883	63.59459	1.20	0.25	2.49	3.80	10.61	0.66	0.27	0.01	1.06	1.37	18.29
RT-11K-4AO1	Type-2 fluorine-rich dike	30.47844	63.59453	0.35	0.06	0.75	5.63	36.17	0.48	3.13	0.00	0.07	0.48	34.98
RT-11K-4AO2	Type-2 fluorine-rich dike	30.47844	63.59453	0.44	0.04	0.88	5.18	23.35	0.84	3.60	0.01	0.09	0.36	24.90
RT-11K-4B3	Type-2 fluorine-rich dike	30.47844	63.59453	0.34	0.05	2.11	5.99	27.16	0.73	0.76	0.00	0.09	0.78	31.77
RT-11K-4C1A	Type-2 fluorine-rich dike	30.47844	63.59453	0.26	0.04	1.06	6.04	27.18	0.71	2.50	0.00	0.07	0.59	27.62
RT-11K-4C1B	Type-2 fluorine-rich dike	30.47844	63.59453	15.55	3.62	8.62	5.80	25.81	0.55	3.90	0.12	4.53	1.22	18.35
RT-11K-5A2	Type-1 concordantly banded REE vein	30.47820	63.59450	0.35	0.06	2.51	6.85	16.87	0.12	0.13	0.00	0.20	1.97	17.98
RT-11K-5A3	Type-1 concordantly banded REE vein	30.47820	63.59450	0.30	0.05	2.59	6.88	17.97	0.16	0.13	0.00	0.60	2.32	18.72
RT-11K-5B1B	Type-1 concordantly banded REE vein	30.47820	63.59450	0.39	0.05	2.79	6.63	16.10	0.19	0.13	0.00	1.29	2.28	18.53
RT-11K-5B3B	Type-1 concordantly banded REE vein	30.47820	63.59450	0.34	0.05	1.81	4.94	20.05	0.13	0.08	0.00	0.54	1.80	16.28
RT-11K-5B6A	Type-1 concordantly banded REE vein	30.47820	63.59450	1.18	0.21	8.14	10.01	20.85	0.10	0.25	0.01	0.09	3.91	27.76
RT-11K-6A2A	Type-2 apatite-rich dike	30.47810	63.59452	16.05	3.59	11.27	10.01	17.39	1.50	4.07	0.14	6.19	1.81	16.29
RT-11K-6A2B	Type-2 apatite-rich dike	30.47810	63.59452	1.01	0.24	5.12	5.10	19.20	4.62	0.40	0.01	3.75	2.12	27.36
RT-11K-6B2	Type-2 apatite-rich dike	30.47810	63.59452	2.11	0.49	6.48	6.86	19.23	3.87	0.64	0.02	1.08	2.58	30.17
RT-11K-6B3	Type-2 apatite-rich dike	30.47810	63.59452	6.50	1.42	7.13	7.00	17.35	3.64	1.73	0.06	3.04	2.06	25.18

17

Unit	Description	Northing	Easting	Trace elements											
				Sc ppm	Be ppm	V ppm	Co ppm	Zn ppm	Ga ppm	Ge ppm	As ppm	Rb ppm	Sr ppm	Y ppm	Zr ppm
RT-11K-1A1	Type-2 fluorine-rich dike	30.47976	63.59494	10	6	20	<1	1,350	75	7	25	4	30,470	108	42
RT-11K-1A2	Type-2 fluorine-rich dike	30.47976	63.59494	10	6	13	<1	1,490	82	8	26	4	39,020	112	23
RT-11K-1B2	Type-2 fluorine-rich dike	30.47976	63.59494	10	6	16	<1	1,370	76	8	27	4	33,570	106	37
RT-11K-2A2	Type-1 concordantly banded REE vein	30.47924	63.59546	11	10	41	2	2,150	50	7	28	<2	22,110	423	147
RT-11K-2B1	Type-1 concordantly banded REE vein	30.47924	63.59546	14	11	43	1	950	65	8	34	<2	38,490	551	148
RT-11K-2B2	Type-1 concordantly banded REE vein	30.47924	63.59546	13	10	39	<1	860	62	8	32	<2	36,380	552	161
RT-11K-3B31	Type-2 patite-rich dike	30.47883	63.59459	25	12	46	2	1,030	71	8	34	6	44,320	454	28
RT-11K-3B32	Type-2 apatite-rich dike	30.47883	63.59459	24	18	43	<1	620	92	8	30	8	60,480	321	21
RT-11K-4AO1	Type-2 fluorine-rich dike	30.47844	63.59453	7	16	44	<1	1,040	45	5	19	<2	47,510	112	33
RT-11K-4AO2	Type-2 fluorine-rich dike	30.47844	63.59453	12	33	74	<1	810	93	7	26	<2	82,400	103	32
RT-11K-4B3	Type-2 fluorine-rich dike	30.47844	63.59453	11	35	108	<1	1,200	77	6	31	<2	70,450	108	22
RT-11K-4C1A	Type-2 fluorine-rich dike	30.47844	63.59453	10	26	52	<1	580	74	6	24	<2	71,960	105	26
RT-11K-4C1B	Type-2 fluorine-rich dike	30.47844	63.59453	6	58	454	5	520	20	3	11	93	19,120	545	82
RT-11K-5A2	Type-1 concordantly banded REE vein	30.47820	63.59450	15	16	26	1	1,210	79	10	37	<2	25,650	465	20
RT-11K-5A3	Type-1 concordantly banded REE vein	30.47820	63.59450	16	15	25	<1	1,050	77	10	34	<2	29,090	540	18
RT-11K-5B1B	Type-1 concordantly banded REE vein	30.47820	63.59450	14	13	25	2	2,260	75	10	38	<2	37,660	575	18
RT-11K-5B3B	Type-1 concordantly banded REE vein	30.47820	63.59450	17	45	39	<1	270	85	11	39	<2	49,520	594	15
RT-11K-5B6A	Type-1 concordantly banded REE vein	30.47820	63.59450	23	40	92	17	2,550	177	18	119	6	49,760	162	21
RT-11K-6A2A	Type-2 apatite-rich dike	30.47810	63.59452	17	25	153	7	1,220	61	8	29	131	23,670	1235	93
RT-11K-6A2B	Type-2 apatite-rich dike	30.47810	63.59452	27	7	27	4	520	165	19	67	8	68,180	677	22
RT-11K-6B2	Type-2 apatite-rich dike	30.47810	63.59452	23	7	42	10	660	139	16	54	15	56,190	314	16
RT-11K-6B3	Type-2 apatite-rich dike	30.47810	63.59452	22	14	61	11	570	136	15	56	51	56,090	706	38

18

Trace elements—Continued

Unit	Description	Northing	Easting	Nb ppm	Mo ppm	Ba ppm	Bi ppm	Lu ppm	Hf ppm	Ta ppm	W ppm	Tl ppm	Pb ppm	Th ppm	U ppm
RT-11K-1A1	Type-2 fluorine-rich dike	30.47976	63.59494	41	5	196,200	<0.4	0.86	0.7	0.3	3	0.9	962	88	15.4
RT-11K-1A2	Type-2 fluorine-rich dike	30.47976	63.59494	52	4	215,100	<0.4	0.91	0.7	0.4	4	0.9	951	99	16.7
RT-11K-1B2	Type-2 fluorine-rich dike	30.47976	63.59494	50	6	187,400	<0.4	0.88	0.8	0.3	3	1.8	885	89	17.5
RT-11K-2A2	Type-1 concordantly banded REE vein	30.47924	63.59546	3	9	190,400	0.6	1.64	1.3	<0.1	4	0.3	991	306	93.2
RT-11K-2B1	Type-1 concordantly banded REE vein	30.47924	63.59546	2	10	207,000	0.5	2.06	1.6	<0.1	4	0.4	784	467	89.7
RT-11K-2B2	Type-1 concordantly banded REE vein	30.47924	63.59546	2	9	210,100	0.5	2.11	1.8	<0.1	4	0.3	748	441	101
RT-11K-3B31	Type-2 patite-rich dike	30.47883	63.59459	83	13	236,300	0.5	1.36	1.2	0.3	3	1.9	390	1,510	29.2
RT-11K-3B32	Type-2 apatite-rich dike	30.47883	63.59459	33	5	285,700	<0.4	0.81	1.1	0.3	3	2	290	1,230	9.8
RT-11K-4AO1	Type-2 fluorine-rich dike	30.47844	63.59453	14	<2	49,850	<0.4	1.34	0.3	0.1	4	0.6	1,210	80	20.7
RT-11K-4AO2	Type-2 fluorine-rich dike	30.47844	63.59453	19	<2	129,200	<0.4	1.21	0.4	0.2	4	0.3	716	108	32.3
RT-11K-4B3	Type-2 fluorine-rich dike	30.47844	63.59453	12	4	106,300	0.6	1.3	0.3	0.2	3	0.7	690	170	31.6
RT-11K-4C1A	Type-2 fluorine-rich dike	30.47844	63.59453	13	<2	106,100	0.4	1.43	0.4	0.2	3	0.4	478	116	27.9
RT-11K-4C1B	Type-2 fluorine-rich dike	30.47844	63.59453	170	4	39,780	3.8	3.53	1.8	4	8	30.2	983	323	172
RT-11K-5A2	Type-1 concordantly banded REE vein	30.47820	63.59450	28	3	245,900	0.9	1.57	1.3	0.4	8	4.5	660	864	8.5
RT-11K-5A3	Type-1 concordantly banded REE vein	30.47820	63.59450	18	3	224,400	0.9	1.67	1.3	0.2	6	1.9	675	869	8.2
RT-11K-5B1B	Type-1 concordantly banded REE vein	30.47820	63.59450	42	3	237,300	1.8	1.8	1.4	0.4	6	2.3	1,420	814	17.6
RT-11K-5B3B	Type-1 concordantly banded REE vein	30.47820	63.59450	72	<2	227,900	<0.4	1.52	1.5	0.2	4	1.1	622	1,070	28.4
RT-11K-5B6A	Type-1 concordantly banded REE vein	30.47820	63.59450	37	11	50,330	1.2	1.36	0.5	2.4	3	2.5	1,950	727	47.6
RT-11K-6A2A	Type-2 apatite-rich dike	30.47810	63.59452	58	10	32,450	7	4.33	2.7	6.5	4	3.3	1,590	438	31.5
RT-11K-6A2B	Type-2 apatite-rich dike	30.47810	63.59452	22	9	87,040	5.3	2.59	1.1	1.5	3	0.6	973	690	37.3
RT-11K-6B2	Type-2 apatite-rich dike	30.47810	63.59452	16	11	74,900	11.3	1.12	0.7	0.8	3	1	1,630	504	15.5
RT-11K-6B3	Type-2 apatite-rich dike	30.47810	63.59452	24	11	69,980	17.8	2.6	1.4	2	4	1.5	3,070	549	22.7

19

Unit	Description	Northing	Easting	REEs												
				La ppm	Ce ppm	Pr ppm	Nd ppm	Sm ppm	Eu ppm	Gd ppm	Tb ppm	Dy ppm	Ho ppm	Er ppm	Tm ppm	Yb ppm
RT-11K-1A1	Type-2 fluorine-rich dike	30.47976	63.59494	10,300	14,600	1,110	2,880	258	40	109	6.9	26.4	3.4	8.3	1.01	5.8
RT-11K-1A2	Type-2 fluorine-rich dike	30.47976	63.59494	11,400	15,800	1,190	3,040	267	41.5	115	7.5	28.4	3.6	8.5	1.06	6.1
RT-11K-1B2	Type-2 fluorine-rich dike	30.47976	63.59494	10,000	14,700	1,160	3,050	278	43.1	109	7.7	28.7	3.5	8.4	1.02	5.7
RT-11K-2A2	Type-1 concordantly banded REE vein	30.47924	63.59546	5,820	8,880	840	2,740	390	74.6	223	27.4	124	15.8	30.5	3.03	14.3
RT-11K-2B1	Type-1 concordantly banded REE vein	30.47924	63.59546	8,620	11,700	1,010	3,090	415	85.1	271	36.5	162	20.8	40.4	3.84	17.1
RT-11K-2B2	Type-1 concordantly banded REE vein	30.47924	63.59546	7,980	11,200	992	3,060	417	84.5	267	36.2	160	20.9	39.8	3.83	16.9
RT-11K-3B31	Type-2 patite-rich dike	30.47883	63.59459	10,400	12,200	945	2,710	445	107	367	47.5	181	18.6	30.9	2.47	11.2
RT-11K-3B32	Type-2 apatite-rich dike	30.47883	63.59459	16,000	16,600	1,180	3,040	328	64.8	221	27	118	13	20.7	1.72	7.1
RT-11K-4AO1	Type-2 fluorine-rich dike	30.47844	63.59453	5,550	7,940	720	2,160	231	37.9	91.7	6.1	22.8	3.1	8.6	1.24	8.4
RT-11K-4AO2	Type-2 fluorine-rich dike	30.47844	63.59453	18,800	17,600	1,170	2,770	217	34.3	108	6.1	23.1	3.3	8.3	1.16	7.4
RT-11K-4B3	Type-2 fluorine-rich dike	30.47844	63.59453	14,500	14,500	1,020	2,540	216	34.3	95.8	5.7	23.1	3.4	9	1.23	7.9
RT-11K-4C1A	Type-2 fluorine-rich dike	30.47844	63.59453	14,100	13,900	995	2,470	210	33.1	90.1	5.3	20.2	3.1	8.4	1.25	8.5
RT-11K-4C1B	Type-2 fluorine-rich dike	30.47844	63.59453	1,440	2,360	244	838	189	48.7	166	24.4	120	18.6	44.3	5.23	27
RT-11K-5A2	Type-1 concordantly banded REE vein	30.47820	63.59450	5,990	13,000	1,240	3,690	507	110	349	44.1	181	19.9	32.8	2.83	12.6
RT-11K-5A3	Type-1 concordantly banded REE vein	30.47820	63.59450	5,870	12,400	1,190	3,580	512	112	369	47.8	201	22.3	36.7	3.29	14
RT-11K-5B1B	Type-1 concordantly banded REE vein	30.47820	63.59450	5,380	11,900	1,180	3,600	508	109	352	46.2	201	23.8	42.3	3.7	15.8
RT-11K-5B3B	Type-1 concordantly banded REE vein	30.47820	63.59450	6,400	13,300	1,270	3,990	626	136	431	55.5	236	25.5	38.2	3.01	12.7
RT-11K-5B6A	Type-1 concordantly banded REE vein	30.47820	63.59450	21,000	31,500	2,600	7,090	657	102	274	15.8	46.5	5	11	1.36	8.3
RT-11K-6A2A	Type-2 apatite-rich dike	30.47810	63.59452	5,790	9,030	870	2,810	397	83.8	279	46.4	266	43.3	98.1	9.48	40.4
RT-11K-6A2B	Type-2 apatite-rich dike	30.47810	63.59452	20,900	29,100	2,480	7,300	816	140	376	37.5	175	25.7	54.6	5.32	23.4
RT-11K-6B2	Type-2 apatite-rich dike	30.47810	63.59452	16,600	23,000	1,980	5,800	615	102	279	22.5	90.8	11.4	22	2.16	9.7
RT-11K-6B3	Type-2 apatite-rich dike	30.47810	63.59452	16,700	22,400	1,890	5,680	660	120	358	38.5	180	26.2	56	5.43	23.1

3.1 Styles of LREE Mineralization

Our first mission through the southern part of LREE zone (August 2010) confirmed the published descriptions of geologic units (Cheremitsyn and Yeremenko, 1976) and identified the presence of fluorite-rich dikes containing abundant REE minerals. Our second mission (February 2011), to the northwest corner of LREE-enriched zone, confirmed the abundance of REE-enriched rocks that are mineralized in two different styles (described below). We also established that the ankerite-barite alvikites, rich in LREE minerals, were emplaced unconformably above normal alvikites, which were already cooled and then intruded by carbonatite dikes before emplacement of LREE-enriched alvikites (fig. 4*B*).

Two styles of REE mineralization occur within ankerite-barite alvikite in the marginal zone of the central vent (fig. 2, Q_{esf}).

Type-1.— Concordant, symmetrically banded veins and seams (fig. 5). Type-1 REE mineralization consists of concordant, symmetrically banded veins and discontinuous seams, as much as 0.5–0.7 m thick and several tens of meters long. The layers of REE enrichment consist of two outer bands of yellow-weathering minerals symmetrically disposed about a dark central band (figs. 5b,c,d). The outer bands of yellow-weathering minerals consist of khanneshite-(Ce), barite, strontianite and secondary synchysite-(Ce) and parisite-(Ce). The dark, central band consists primarily of ankeritic-dolomite, barite, apatite, and strontianite; trace khanneshite-(Ce) is present as well. These banded rocks, highly enriched in REE, are interlayered with weakly mineralized ankerite-barite alvikite (that is, the host well-rocks) for more than 150 meters of exposed vertical section.

Type-2.—Discordant tabular sheets (fig. 6). Type-2 REE mineralization occurs as discordant dikes and tabular sheets composed of primary igneous minerals that crystallized directly from magma or a late-stage hydrothermal fluid (fig. 6 *A,B,C,H*). These REE-enriched igneous dikes are of two types that are identifiable in the field by their major minerals and phenocryst assemblages: (1) those enriched in fluorine and (2) those enriched in phosphorus. The igneous dikes enriched in fluorine contain idiomorphic phenocrysts of khanneshite-(Ce) or pseudomorphs of yellow-weathering REE-carbonates (fig. 6*F*), with or without fluorite (fig. 6*G*); in addition, synchysite-(Ce), bastnäsite-(Ce), and calkinsite-(Ce), of likely secondary origin (hydrothermal alteration), may also be present. The igneous dikes enriched in phosphorus contain idiomorphic phenocrysts of carbocernaite-(Ce) and apatite (fig. 6,*D,E*); in addition, parisite-(Ce) of likely secondary origin, may also be present. Both types of igneous dikes occur at many scales throughout the zone of LREE enrichment. Most dikes are 50–60 cm thick and traceable for tens of meters; others are 10–50 meters thick and traceable for hundreds of meters (Cheremitsyn and Yeremenko, 1976).

3.2 Whole-Rock Geochemistry

Tables 1–3 present major-, trace-, and rare earth element concentration data for representative rocks from the Khanneshin carbonatite complex. There is strong geologic evidence for multiple generations of igneous rock and at least two or more types of distinctive carbonatite magma. Soviet geologists first identified two sequences of volcanic strata (fig. 2, Q_{1-1} and Q_{1-3}) that are separated by a sequence of volcano-sedimentary rocks (Q_{1-2}). These stratified rocks, in turn, are intruded by several small hypabyssal intrusions (Q_{aa}) and numerous carbonatite dikes with crude radial geometry (fig. 2). Moreover, in the critical zone of LREE enrichment, several outcrops demonstrate that the barite-strontianite alvikites, rich in LREE minerals, were emplaced above an older section of ankerite alvikite that had already been cooled and intruded by dikes of carbonatite (ig. 2, Q_{esf}; fig. 4*B*).

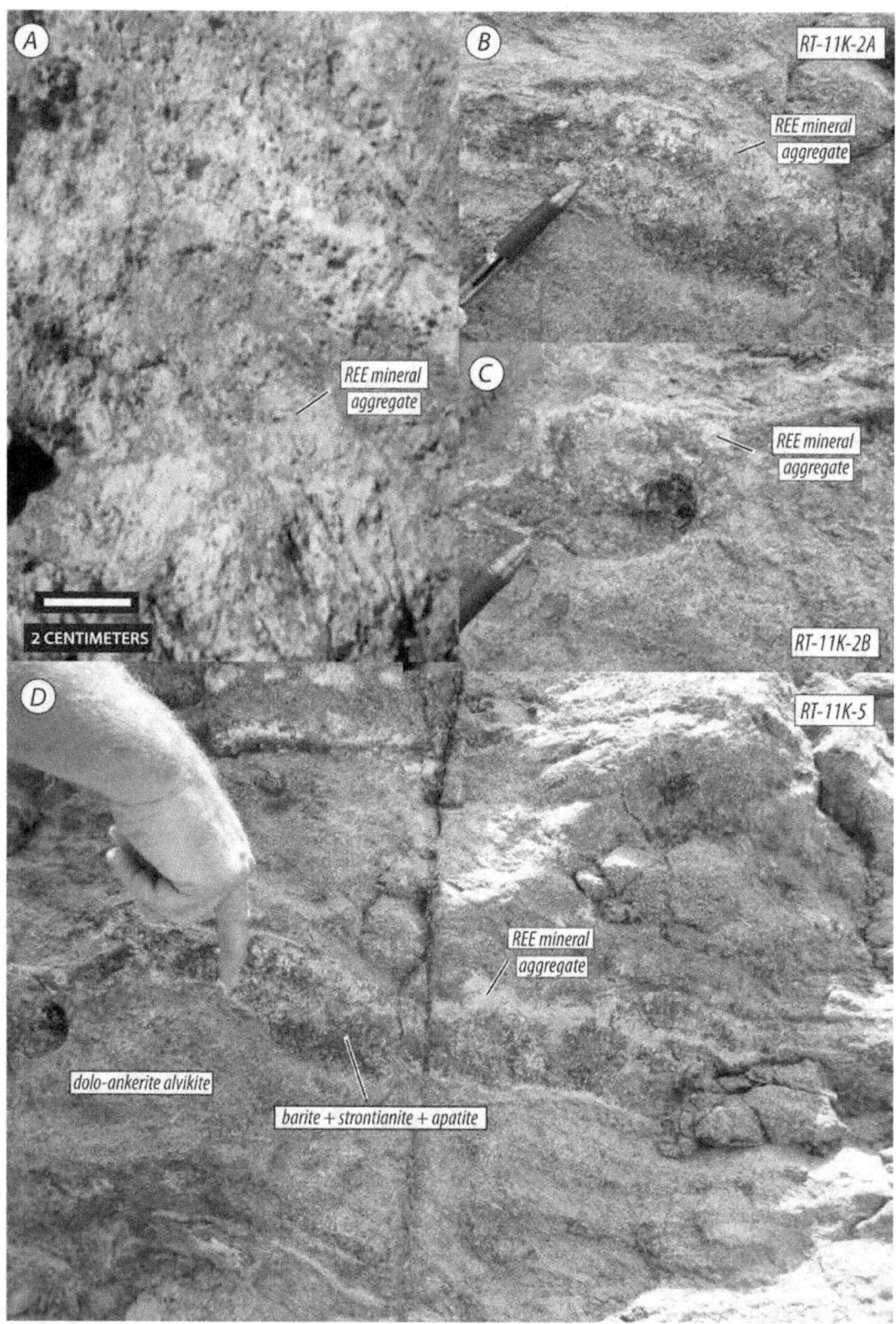

Figure 5. Photographs of examples of type-1 rare earth element (REE) mineralization in the marginal zone of the intrusive central vent (traverse 3, fig. 2), Khanneshin carbonatite complex, Afghanistan. *A*, Medium-grained alvikite

in the zone of light rare earth element (LREE) enrichment with characteristic yellow-weathering indicating the presence of LREE-carbonate minerals. *B*, A seam of type-1 mineralization showing the symmetric, banded nature of LREE-rich alvikite (sample RT-11K-2A). *C*, Photograph of a partially rotated type-1 vein, suggesting great fluidity of the mineralized rocks (sample RT-11K-2B). *D*, Dolomite-ankerite (dolo-ankerite) alvikite and type-1 mineral bands at station RT-11K-5. The symmetrically banded seams of mineralized alvikite are centimeters thick; they consist of two outer bands, enriched in LREE-carbonate minerals, and a dark central band of barite-strontianite-apatite alvikite. These mineral bands alternate, on the scale of centimeters, with typical dolomite-ankerite alvikite, over a vertical thickness of approximately 150 m.

These observations are borne out by our geochemical data that indicate major differences in chemistry between rocks of the southwestern and northeastern part of the complex (fig. 7). The carbonatite dikes and tuffs from the southwest part of the complex (traverse 1A, B) are silico-carbonatites (~21 wt. percent SiO_2, table 1), having generally low MgO contents (~2.4 average wt. percent, fig. 7a). In contrast, LREE-enriched alvikites from the northeast margin of the central vent are mostly ferro- and magnesio-carbonatites (fig. 7*B*), having relatively low SiO_2 contents (~2.3 average wt. percent, table 3). The latter group of rocks, particularly the type-2 discordant igneous dikes, grade into true calico-carbonatites (fig. 7*A*).

Other chemical characteristics of the Khanneshin complex include the following:

1. LREE-enriched alvikites of the central vent contain as much as 10 wt. percent MnO (table 3, fig. 8*A*), and they are composed of manganiferous minerals such as manganoan ankerite, ferroan rhodochrosite, pyrolusite, and manganosite.

2. Strontium (Sr) and barium (Ba), commonly present as trace elements in many carbonatite massifs, are greatly enriched in LREE-enriched rocks of the Khanneshin complex. In typical alvikite and sövite of the volcanic apron and central vent (tables 1 and 2), Sr and Ba average 10,000 ppm and 3,000 ppm, respectively. In LREE-enriched zone of the central vent (table 3), the barite-strontianite alvikites average 4.5 wt. percent Sr (45,000 ppm), and 15.5 wt. percent Ba (155,000 ppm). In rare instances, whole-rock concentrations of Sr and Ba in LREE-enriched rocks exceed 82,000 and 280,000 ppm, respectively (table 4). Figures 8*B* and *C* illustrate the high content of Sr and Ba in alvikite of LREE-enriched zone over average ferro-, magnesio-, and calico-carbonatite. Also shown in figure 8*C* are whole-rock analyses of a carbonatite dike and mineralized carbonate at Bayan Obo, China.

3. In addition to Sr and Ba, the LREE zone is extraordinarily enriched in F and S, which is indicated by the ubiquitous presence of fluorite, barite, and less commonly, celestine.

4. In common with carbonatites in general, the igneous rocks from the Khanneshin complex are strongly enriched in the LREE over HREE. Within the population of REE-enriched rocks, however, there is a positive correlation between the concentration of P and HREE. This relationship is particularly apparent for the type-1 mineralized alvikites which contain abundant apatite and as much as 40 ppm Yb, a proxy for the HREE (fig. 8*D*). Type-2 igneous dikes, however, are depleted in apatite (having 0.1–0.3 wt. percent P_2O_5) and contain less than 10 ppm Yb. Thus it would appear that apatite, not a REE-carbonate, is the principal carrier of the HREE in the type-1 alvikites.

5. Both type-1 and type-2 mineralized rocks have REE concentrations that approach world-class levels of enrichment. Figure 9 illustrates the concentration values of REE-enriched rocks from Khanneshin together with the ores from Mountain Pass, Calif., and Bayan Obo, China. The most REE-enriched samples from Khanneshin, which include both type-1 and type-2 mineralized

rocks, range in $\sum$ LREE concentration (the sum of La, Ce, Pr, and Nd) between 0.488–6.219 wt. percent with an average value of 3.063 wt. percent (table 4). Of these, type-1 mineralized rocks have an average $\sum$ LREE value of 2.775 wt. percent, with a range for eight samples between 6.219 and 1.826 wt. percent. Type-2 mineralized rocks have an average $\sum$ LREE value of 3.282 wt. percent, with a range for 14 samples between 5.978 and 0.488 wt. percent. Although the absolute concentrations of the HREE are low relative to LREE, the HREE values of the type-1 and type-2 mineralized rocks are high relative to the ores from Bayan Obo and Mountain Pass ores (fig. 9).

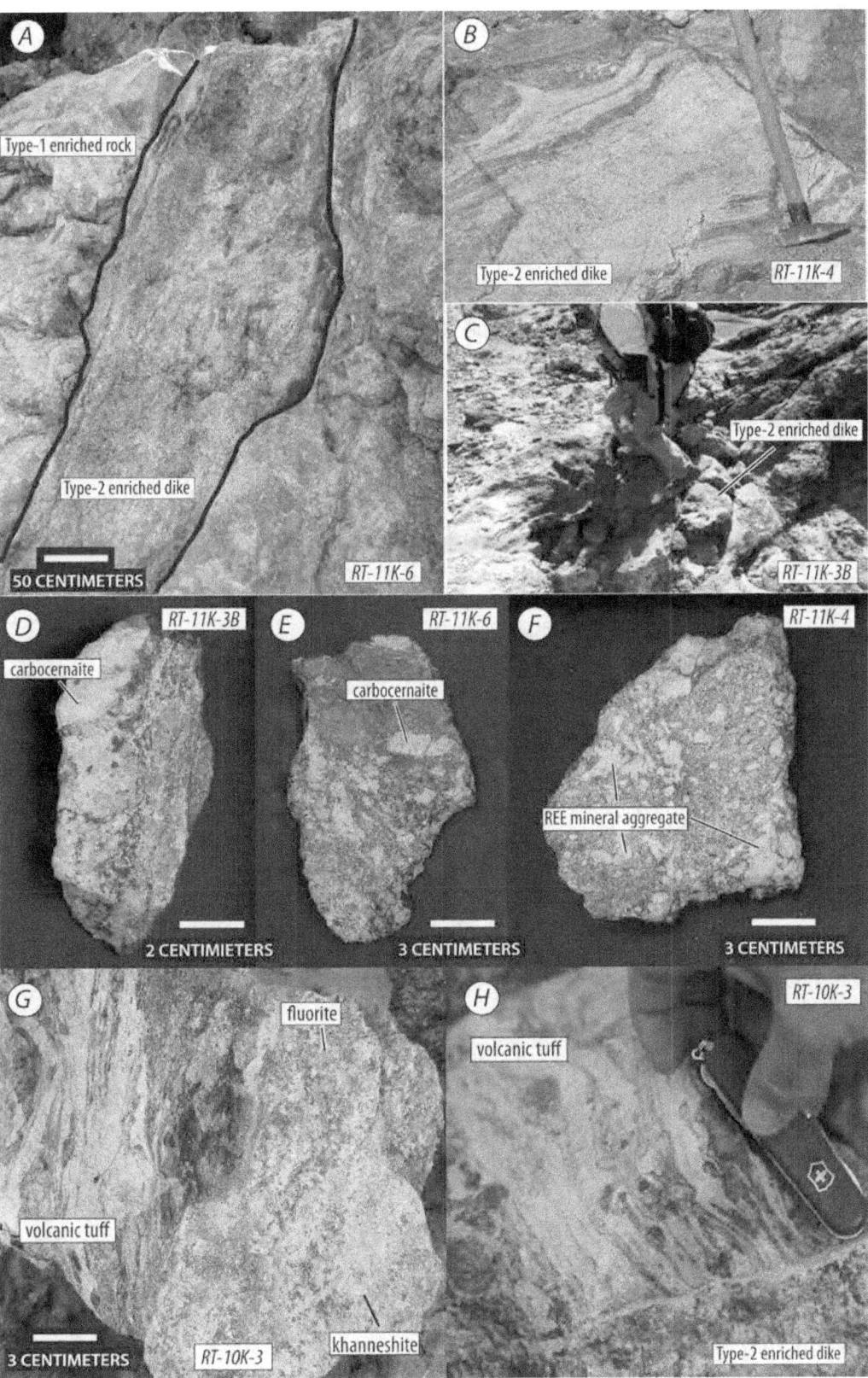

Figure 6 (on previous page). Photographs of examples of type-2 mineralized dikes in the zone of light rare earth element (LREE) enrichment (traverse 3, fig. 2), Khanneshin carbonatite complex, Afghanistan. *A*, Apatite-rich carbonatite dike, with local igneous, pegmatitic texture, at field station RT-11K-6. The carbonatite dike, approximately 75 cm thick and steeply dipping, intrudes the concordantly banded type-1 mineralized alvikite (top left of the figure). *B*, Fluorine-rich carbonatite dike (RT-11K-4) that intrudes the banded alvikites of the marginal zone, intrusive central vent. *C*, A thin apatite-rich dike (under the hiker's foot) intruding yellow-weathering REE-enriched alvikite of the marginal zone, intrusive central vent (RT-11K-3B). *D*, Rock-slab of the apatite-rich carbonatite dike, RT-11K-3B, showing the large phenocrysts of carbocernaite in a matrix of dolomitic-ankerite, apatite, barite, and strontianite. *E*, Rock-slab of the apatite-rich carbonatite dike, RT-11K-6, showing the large phenocrysts of carbocernaite in a matrix of dolomitic-ankerite, apatite, barite, and strontianite. *F*, Slab of the fluorine-rich carbonatite dike, RT-11K-4, showing the large phenocrysts of LREE-carbonate in a fine-grained matrix of dolomite, barite, strontianite, and calcite. Also present, but too small to see at this scale, are phenocrysts of a former fluorine-bearing mineral now pseudomorphed by a Sr-rich orthocarbonate and an unidentified compound with K, Mg and F. *G*, Hand-specimen of a fluorite- and khanneshite-bearing carbonatite dike (RT-10K-3, traverse 2) that has intruded discordantly across the layering of the host volcanic tuff (alvikite). *H*, Close-up of the fluorine-rich dike (RT-10K-3) and its contact with the layered volcanic tuff.

Table 4. Table of minerals containing rare earth elements (REE), Sr, and Ba as major elements, Khanneshin carbonatite complex, Afghanistan.

[wt. %, weight percent]

Mineral	Formula	Theoretical REE_2O_3 (wt.%)[1]
Khanneshite-(Ce)	$(Na,Ca)_3 (Ce,Ba,Sr)_3(CO_3)_5$	8.03
Carbocernaite-(Ce)	$(Ca,Na)(Sr,Ce,Ba)(CO_3)_2$	18.64
Ancylite-(Ce)	$Sr(Ce) (CO_3)_2 (OH) \cdot H_2O$	42.87
Calkinsite-(Ce)	$(Ce,La)_2 (CO_3)_3 . 4H_2O$	39.53
Synchysite-(Ce)	$Ca(Ce,La)(CO_3)_2F$	43.89
Parisite-(Ce)	$Ca(Ce,La)_2(CO_3)_3F_2$	33.60
Bastnäsite-(Ce)	$(Ce, La) CO_3 F$	74.90
Monazite-(Ce)	$(Ce,La,Th)PO_4$	51.11
Belovite-(Ce)	$(Sr,Ce,Na,Ca)_5(PO_4)_3(OH)$	32.98
Apatite-(Ce)	$(Ca,Ce)_5PO_3F$	<1.00
Strontianite	$SrCO_3$	
Barite	$BaSO_4$	
Celestine	$SrSO_4$	

[1]*http://webmineral.com/data/.*

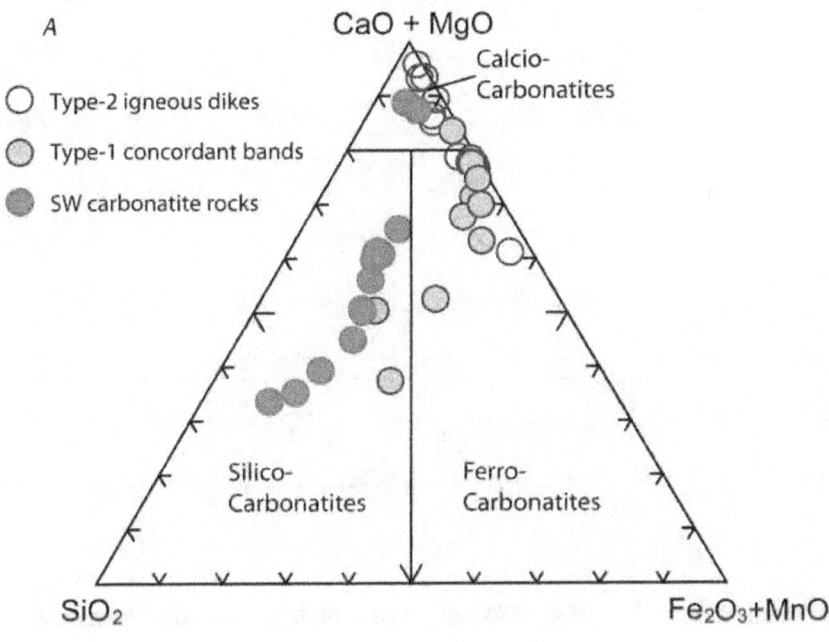

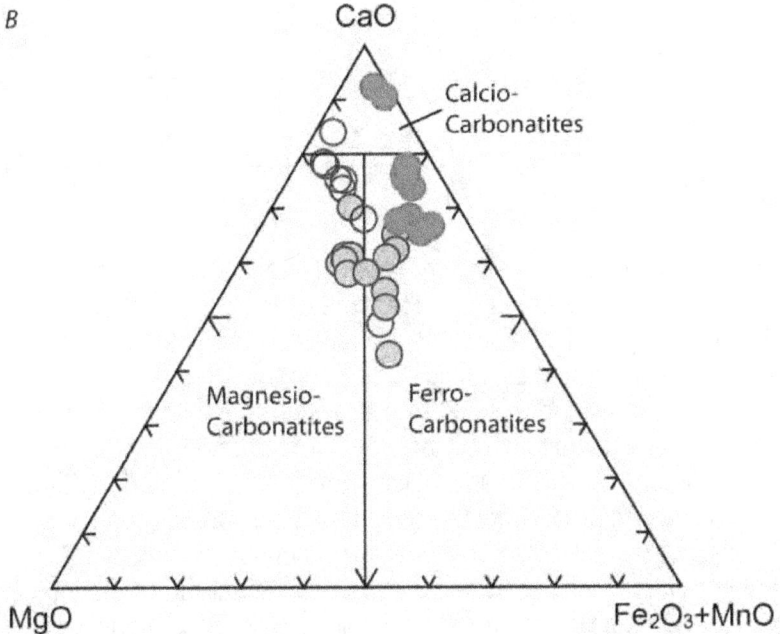

Figure 7. Ternary diagrams of major-element concentration data, Khanneshin carbonatite complex, Afghanistan. Note the distinctive difference between samples from different parts of the complex. Red circles are volcanic strata and minor intrusive rocks from the southwest part of the complex (fig. 2, traverse 1A and B). Filled blue circles are type-1 mineralized rocks; open blue circles are type-2 mineralized dikes (fig. 2, traverse 3). A, Type-1 and -2 mineralized rocks from the zone of LREE enrichment are noticeably depleted in silica, relative to the volcanic rocks and dikes from southwest part of the complex. B, Type-1 and -2 mineralized rocks are also noticeably enriched in MgO relative to the volcanic rocks and dikes from southwest part of the complex. Field boundaries of silico-, ferro-, calico-, and magnesio-carbonatite after Srivastava (1993) and Woolley and Kempe (1989).

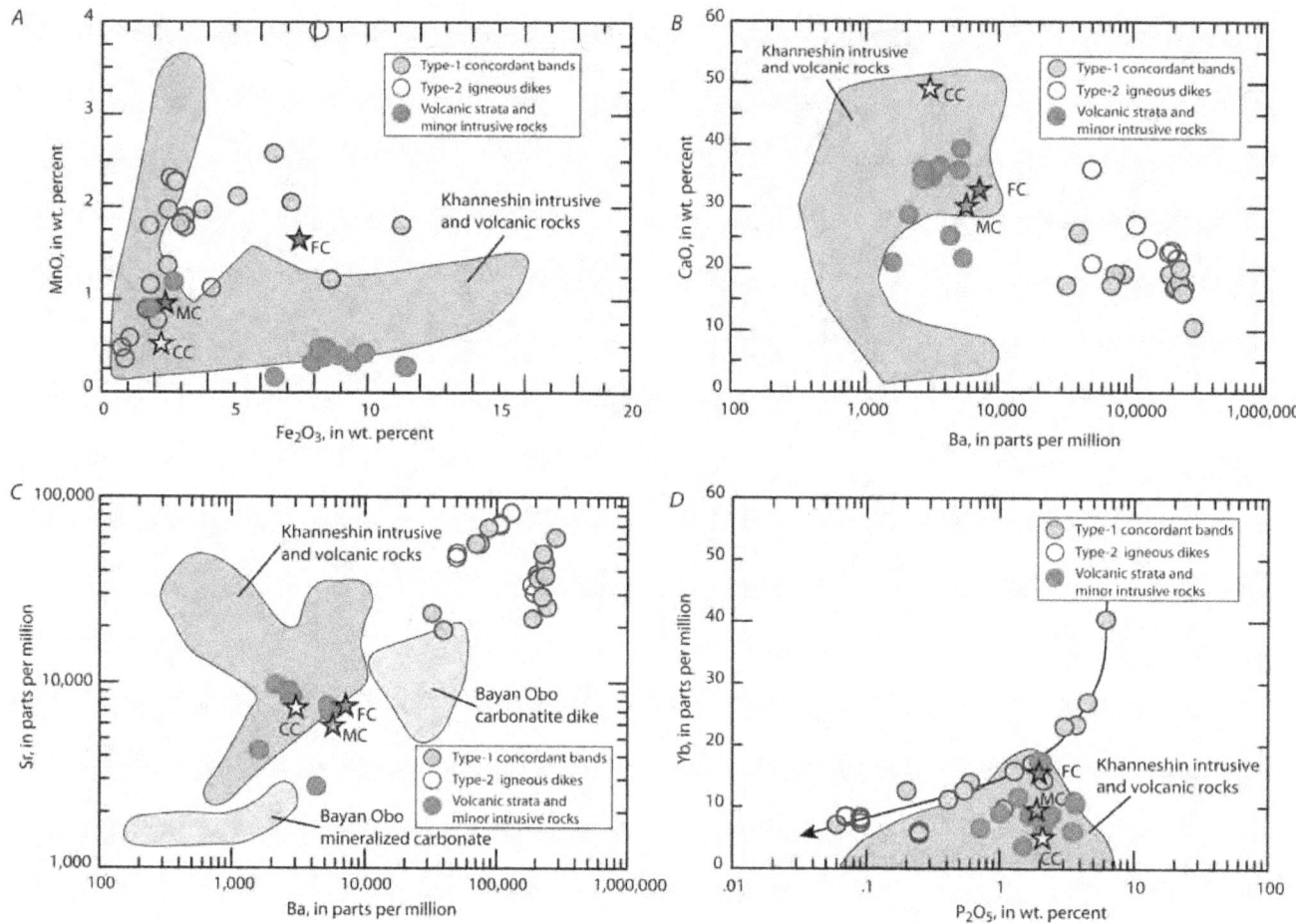

Figure 8. Variation diagrams illustrating the difference in major- and trace-element concentrations among igneous rocks of the, Khanneshin carbonatite complex, Afghanistan. Red circles are volcanic strata and minor intrusive rocks from the southwest part of the complex (fig. 2, traverse 1A and B). Filled blue circles are type-1 mineralized rocks; open blue circles are type-2 mineralized dikes (fig. 2, traverse 3). The orange field delineates the intrusive and extrusive igneous rocks from traverses 1 and 2 (fig. 2). Average values of calico-carbonatite (yellow star), ferro-carbonatite (red star), and magnesio-carbonatite (blue star) from Woolley and Kempe (1989). *A*, MnO versus Fe_2O_3 (weight percent). Note the strong enrichment in MnO of light rare earth element (LREE)- enriched rocks over common alvikite of the Khanneshin complex. *B*, CaO (weight percent) versus Ba (parts per million) (1 percent (parts per hundred) equals 10,000 parts per million). Note the very high concentrations of Ba, relative to CaO in LREE-enriched rocks of the Khanneshin complex. *C*, Sr versus Ba (parts per million). Note the very high concentrations of Ba relative to Sr in LREE-enriched rocks of the Khanneshin complex. Also shown are concentrations in carbonatite dike at Bayan Obo (China) (data from Yang and others, 2009). *D*, Yb (parts per million) versus log P_2O_5 (weight percent). Note the strong correlation between Yb and P_2O_5 in LREE-enriched rocks of the Khanneshin complex suggesting that apatite controls the abundance of HREE. The type-1 mineralized rocks, and those type-2 intrusive dikes having modal apatite and carbocernaite, are enriched in Yb and the heavy rare earth elements (HREE). The fluorine-rich type-2 dikes, bearing either fluorite or the unnamed K-Mg-F phase, are poor in apatite and HREE.

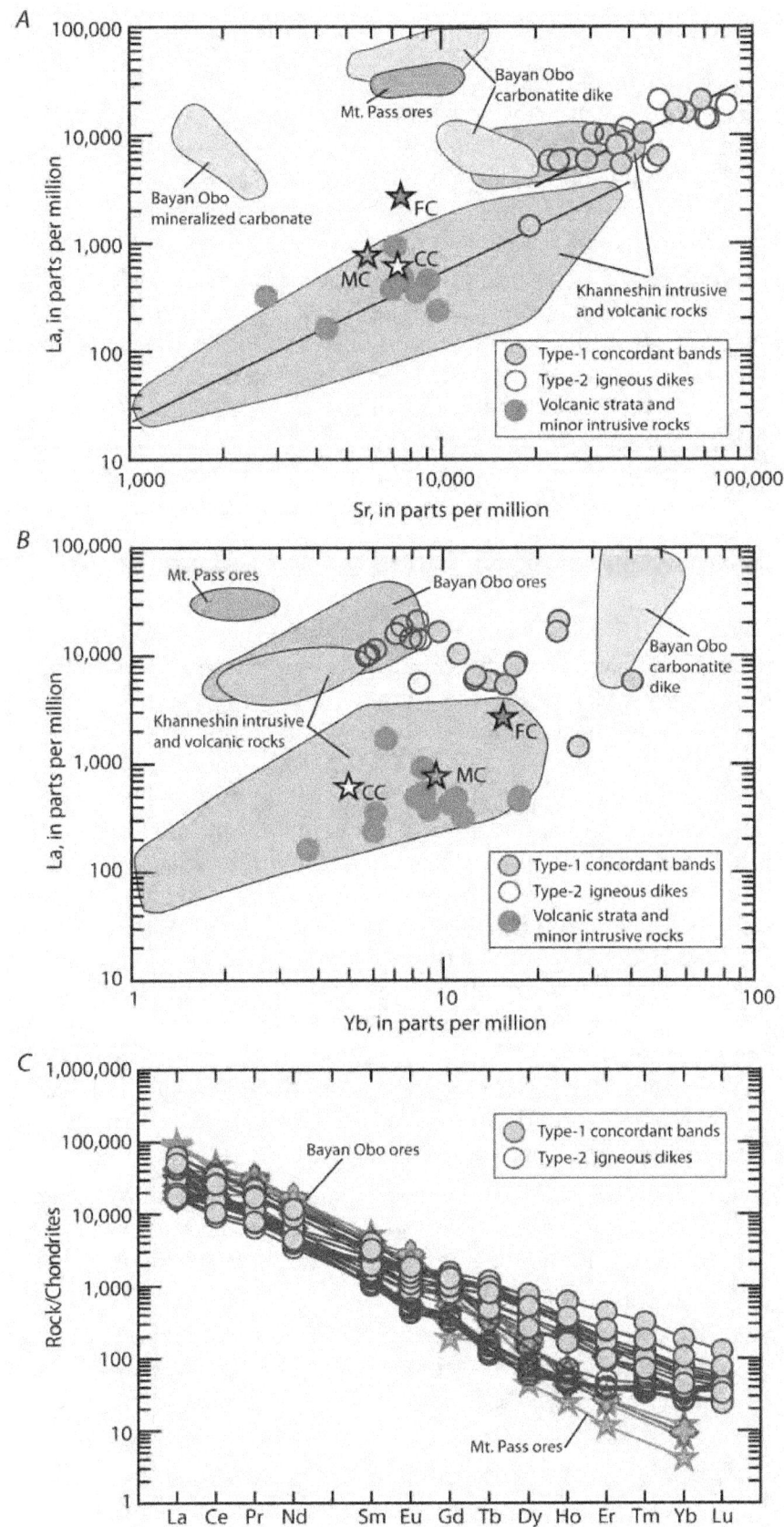

A

La, in parts per million (vertical axis): 10, 100, 1,000, 10,000, 100,000
Sr, in parts per million (horizontal axis): 1,000, 10,000, 100,000

Bayan Obo carbonatite dike
Mt. Pass ores
Bayan Obo mineralized carbonate
FC
MC
CC
Khanneshin intrusive and volcanic rocks

Type-1 concordant bands
Type-2 igneous dikes
Volcanic strata and minor intrusive rocks

B

La, in parts per million (vertical axis): 10, 100, 1,000, 10,000, 100,000
Yb, in parts per million (horizontal axis): 1, 10, 100

Mt. Pass ores
Bayan Obo ores
Bayan Obo carbonatite dike
Khanneshin intrusive and volcanic rocks
FC
MC
CC

Type-1 concordant bands
Type-2 igneous dikes
Volcanic strata and minor intrusive rocks

C

Rock/Chondrites (vertical axis): 1, 10, 100, 1,000, 10,000, 100,000, 1,000,000
La Ce Pr Nd Sm Eu Gd Tb Dy Ho Er Tm Yb Lu

Bayan Obo ores
Mt. Pass ores

Type-1 concordant bands
Type-2 igneous dikes

29

Figure 9 (on previous page).   Graphs showing the magnitude of rare earth element (REE) enrichment in the marginal zone, intrusive central vent, Khanneshin carbonatite complex, Afghanistan. Red circles are volcanic strata and minor intrusive rocks from the southwest part of the complex (fig. 2, traverse 1A and B). Filled blue circles are type-1 mineralized rocks; open blue circles are type-2 mineralized dikes (fig. 2, traverse 3). Average values of calico-carbonatite (yellow star), ferro-carbonatite (red star), and magnesio-carbonatite (blue star) from Woolley and Kempe (1989). *A*, La, representative of light rare earth elements (LREE), versus Sr, in parts per million (ppm). The positive correlation of LREE and Sr in REE-enriched rocks indicates the propensity of LREE to substitute for Sr in khanneshite-(Ce) (burbankite group) and carbocernaite, the primary carbonate minerals of the Khanneshin complex. Also shown are mineralized carbonate and carbonatite dikes from Bayan Obo, China (data from Yang and others, 2009), and average ores from Mountain Pass, Calif. (data from Castor, 2008). *B*, La, representative of LREE, versus Yb, representative of the HREE (in ppm). Common alvikites of the Khanneshin complex have LREE and HREE (heavy rare earth element) concentrations similar to average ferro-, magnesio-, and calcio-carbonatites world-wide. Type-1 and -2 igneous rocks of the Khanneshin complex (filled and open blue circles) are highly enriched in REE and comparable in grade to the world-class REE deposits of Bayan Obo (data for average Bayan Obo ores from Yuan and others, 1992) and Mountain Pass (data from Castor, 2008). *C*, Type-1 and type-2 mineralized rocks from the Khanneshin complex normalized relative to chondrite values (Nakamura, 1974). Also shown are REE ores from Mountain Pass (blue stars) and Bayan Obo (data sources as in *B*).

3.3 Mineralogy

Identification and description of LREE minerals is difficult because of their fine-grained size, altered and pseudomorphed appearance, complex chemistry (allowable coupled substitutions and solid solutions), and extensive polymorphism. As a result LREE-bearing minerals have variable physical and optical properties that make their identification nearly impossible by standard optical petrographic means.

The REE-bearing minerals in our samples were examined using energy-dispersive X-ray spectroscopy (EDS) and back-scattered electron imaging at the electron microscope and microprobe facility, National Center, U.S. Geological Survey, Reston, Virginia. During EDS, a sample is exposed to a beam of electrons that collide with electrons within the sample, causing some of the latter to be knocked out of their orbits. The vacated positions are filled by higher energy electrons that emit x-rays in the process. Our JEOL JXA-8900R scanning electron microprobe is equipped with a Si(Li) EDS Noran Instrument detector with a nominal resolution of 138 electron volts (eV). For additional confirmation for elements such as F and Ce, appropriate wave-length dispersive X-ray spectrometers were peaked-up on standards of known composition. Difficulties that may arise from EDS analysis include the inability to determine water and carbon dioxide content, loss of Na and F under the electron beam, and subtle interferences of the major and secondary peaks of Ba with REE.

The key mineralogical features and associations in REE enriched rocks (table 4) are:

1. In the concordantly banded rocks, LREE minerals formed late in the mineral paragenesis; they are commonly seen as interstitial crystals, late-forming overgrowths on carbonate species, or as spheroidal and anhedral mineral aggregrates perhaps crystallizing as late-generation immiscible droplets (figs. 10 and 11).

2. In the discordant dikes, LREE minerals are present as euhedral to subhedral phenocrysts that crystallized early in the petrogenetic sequence. Commonly the early phenocrysts are altered or pseudomorphed by secondary minerals, including synchysite-(Ce), strontianite, and barite (figs. 12, 13, 14).

3. LREE-enriched rocks contain either fluorite or apatite. In a single instance, an unidentified mineral was found, composed of potassium, magnesium, and fluorine (possibly $KMgF_3$,

analogous with neighborite); its crystallographic structure has yet to be determined (fig. 13*F*).

4. The principal LREE- minerals in the fluorine-rich rocks are khanneshite-(Ce) or monazite-(Ce), which may or may not be pseudomorphed by synchysite-(Ce), barite, and strontianite (figs. 13*C,D*). Bastnäsite-(Ce) and calkinsite-(Ce) are also present in these rocks, commonly as late alteration minerals growing over khanneshite-(Ce) or calcite. On the basis of our limited field work, all rocks rich in fluorine occur as late intrusive dikes and tabular sheets, which are meters wide and scores of meters long. Cheremitsyn and Yeremenko (1976), who first identified REE-enriched dikes, report them as steeply dipping sheets of variable strike that range in thickness and length between 20–60 m and 50-500 m, respectively.

5. A second suite of igneous dikes contain abundant apatite and lack modal fluoride minerals. In this suite, carbocernaite is the primary LREE mineral and forms large (20–100 mm) idiomorphic phenocrysts, constituting as much as 20 modal percent of the rock (fig. 14). Rocks containing carbocernaite are characterized by moderately high P_2O_5 contents (1.08–6.19 wt. percent) and high Na contents (3.64–4.6 wt. percent). Like the fluorine-rich dikes, igneous dikes of the second suite form steeply dipping sheets of variable strike that range in thickness and length from 0.5–2 m to 10–50 m, respectively.

6. All of the concordantly banded rocks are rich in apatite and lack fluorite. The concordantly banded nature of these rocks is defined by a dark, central layer, centimeters thick, of ankeritic dolomite, together with siderite and interstitial barite, strontianite, apatite, and calcite (figs. 10*A*, 11*A*). Khanneshite-(Ce), barite, and strontianite form the outer light-colored bands, which are millimeters thick and symmetrically disposed about the dark central layer. In thin section, the outer band of khanneshite-(Ce), barite, and strontianite displays a brecciated texture against the central band of dolomitic ankerite. This may suggest that a hydrothermal fluid, or fluid-rich magma rich in LREE, Ba, Sr, and P, was introduced into the ankeritic alvikite late in the petrogenetic history. In many instances, khanneshite-(Ce) in the outer band forms unusual spherical aggregates, approximately 100 micrometers in diameter, suggesting that it crystallized as immiscible LREE-enriched droplets in the late-stage liquid.

7. The hypothesis of a late-stage liquid, enriched in LREE, is compatible with other observations. Two suites of dikes of different composition intrude the concordantly banded LREE-enriched rocks. Type-2 igneous dikes include those enriched in P_2O_5, and hence modal apatite, and those enriched in F, and hence modal fluorite or another F-bearing mineral. Thus, there is abundant evidence, both geological and mineralogical, that introduction of REE was a late-stage phenomena that also includes enrichment of fluorine, phosphorus, Ba, and Sr. In our opinion, it is conceivable that both styles of LREE mineralization are penecontemporaneous, having formed in the marginal zone of carbonate-rich magma, highly charged with volatile constituents (F, CO_2, and P_2O_5) and strongly enriched in Ba, Sr, and LREE.

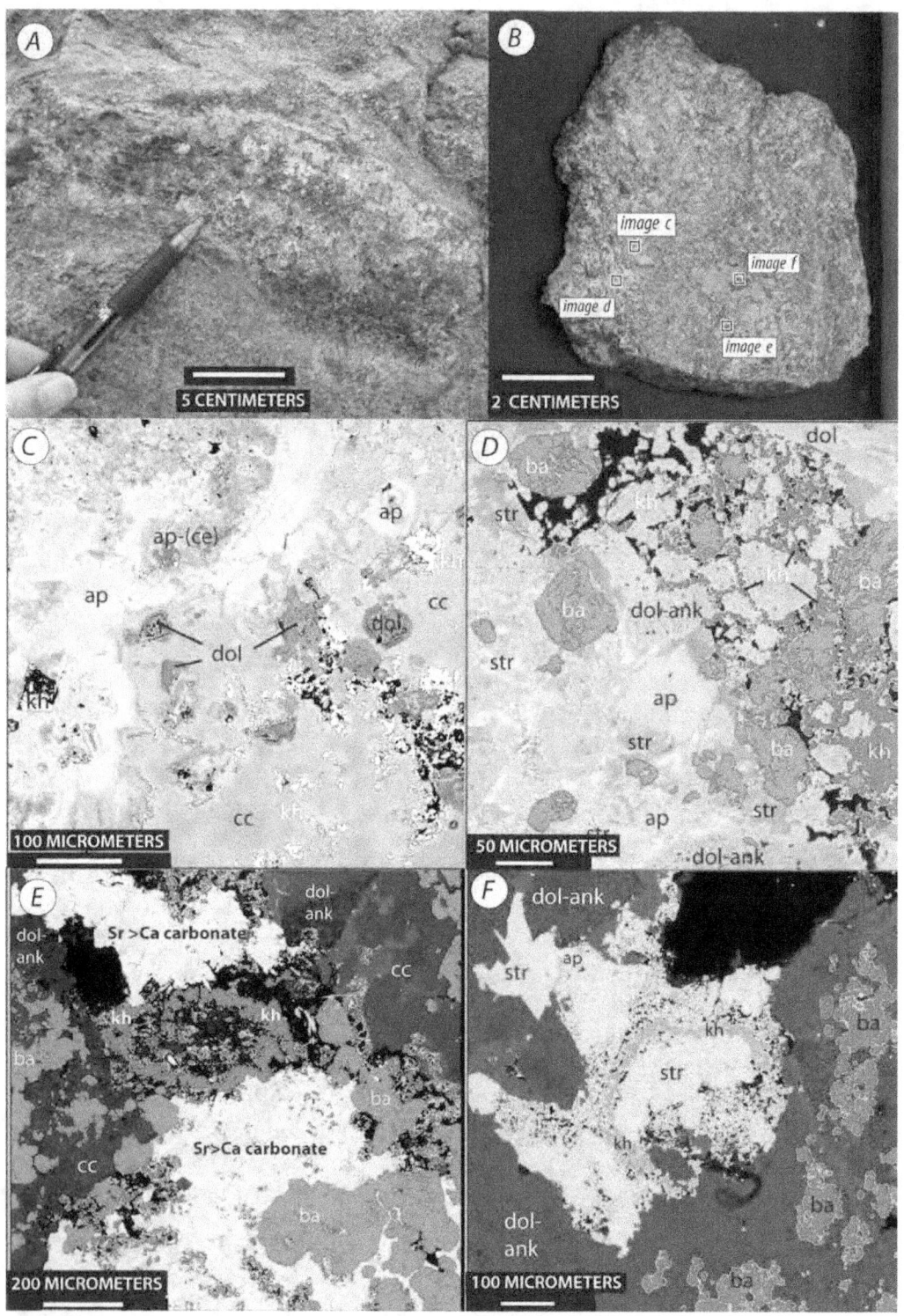

Figure 10.   Mineralogy and crystallization sequence of sample RT-11K-2, type-1 mineralization, Khanneshin carbonatite complex, Afghanistan. *A*, Photograph of the type-1 mineral bands in dolomitic alvikite. *B*, Slab of the symmetrically zoned band, identified in *A*, showing the location of the false-colored, backscattered electron images (*C–F*). *C*, False-colored backscattered electron image within the dark band consisting of apatite, dolomite, calcite,

and trace khanneshite-(Ce): apatite (ap), apatite-(Ce) (ap-(Ce)), dolomite (dol), khanneshite-(Ce) (kh), and calcite (cc). Calcite and khanneshite-(Ce) appear as late, interstitial minerals enclosing early formed phenocrysts of dolomite and apatite. *D*, False-colored backscattered electron image: dolomitic ankerite (dol-ank), apatite (ap), barite (ba), strontianite (str), and khanneshite-(Ce) (kh). Barite, strontianite, and khanneshite appear as an infilling of late minerals into brecciated dolomitic ankerite of the host alvikite. *E*, False-colored backscattered electron image, light-colored band: Sr-rich orthocarbonate (Sr >Ca carbonate), barite (ba), dolomitic-ankerite (dol-ank), calcite (cc), khanneshite (kh). *F*, False-colored backscattered electron image, dark-colored band: barite (ba), dolomitic-ankerite (dol-ank), apatite (ap), strontianite (str) and khanneshite-(Ce) (kh). Dark bands consist mostly of dolomitic ankerite and barite with interstitial strontianite, apatite, and spherical areas (immiscible droplets?) of khanneshite-(Ce) and strontianite.

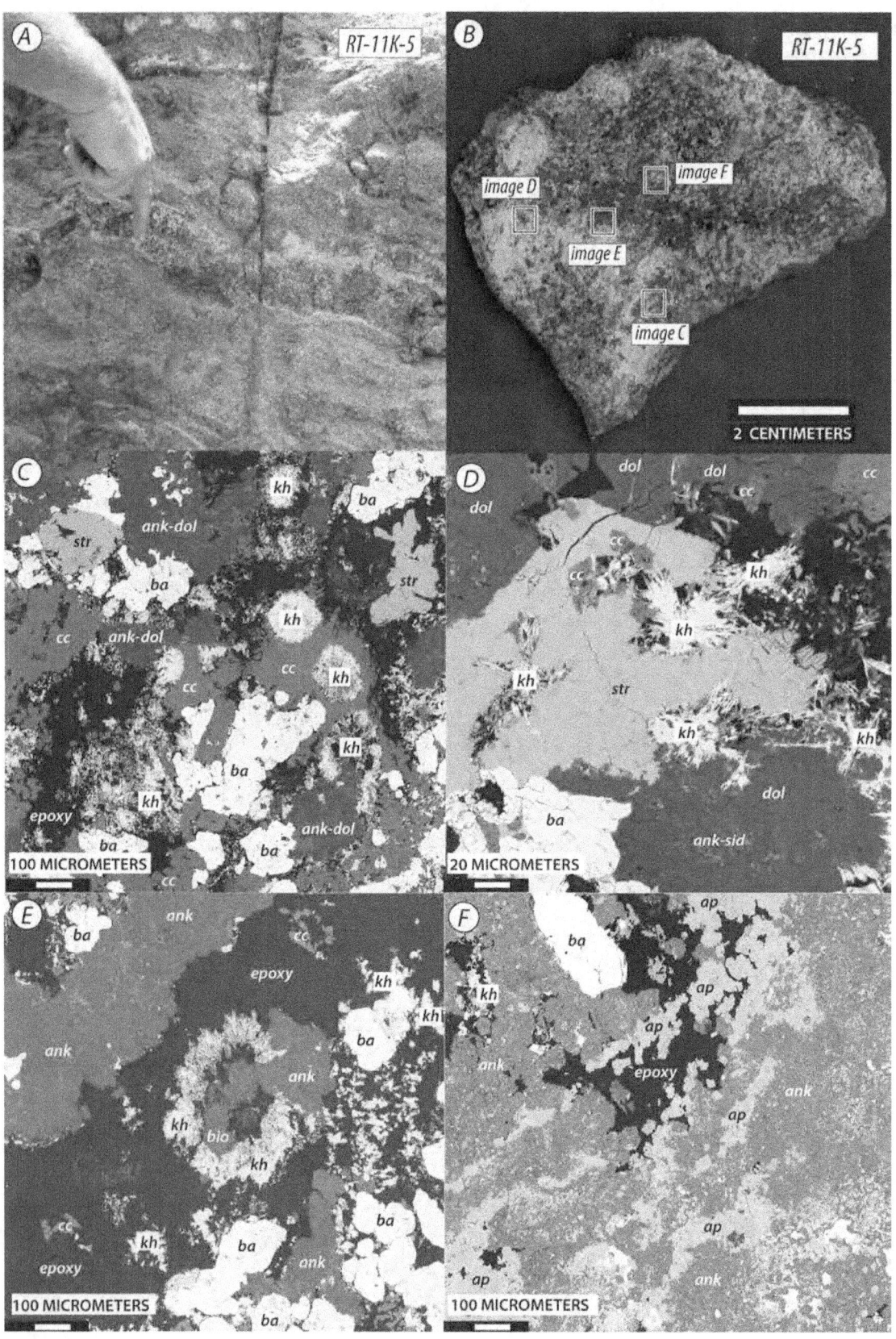

Figure 11 (on previous page). Mineralogy and crystallization sequence of sample RT-11K-5, type-1 mineralization, Khanneshin carbonatite complex, Afghanistan. *A*, Photograph of the type-1 mineral bands in dolomitic alvikite. *B*, Slab of the symmetrically zoned band, identified in *A*, showing the (approximate) location of false-colored, backscattered electron images (*C–F*). *C*, Gray-toned backscattered electron image, margin of light-colored band of ankeritic-dolomite shown in *B*, consisting of barite, strontianite, calcite, and spherical areas (immiscible droplets?) of khanneshite-(Ce): barite (ba), strontianite (str), calcite (cc), ankeritic-dolomite (ank-dol), khanneshite-(Ce) (kh). Calcite and khanneshite-(Ce) appear as late, interstitial minerals enclosing early formed phenocrysts of barite and strontianite. *D*, Gray-toned backscattered electron image, light-colored band shown in *B*: dolomite (dol) with ankeritic-siderite core (ank-sid), barite (ba), strontianite (str), calcite (cc), and khanneshite-(Ce) (kh). Ankeritic-siderite, dolomite, and barite are early phenocrysts, whereas strontianite and calcite are interstitial minerals; khanneshite-(Ce) appears as a late overgrowth (alteration mineral) on calcite. *E*, Gray-toned backscattered electron image, light-colored band shown in *B*: ankerite (ank), barite (ba), biotite (bio), calcite (cc), and khanneshite-(Ce) (kh). Khanneshite-(Ce) appears to have crystallized as an aggregate assemblage, rich in silica, within an interstitial zone of calcite. In the center of the khanneshite aggregate is a crystal of biotite. *F*, Gray-toned backscattered electron image, dark-colored band shown in *B*: ankerite (ank), barite (ba), and apatite (ap). The dark bands consist mostly of ankerite and barite with interstitial apatite.

Figure 12. Mineralogy and crystallization sequence of fluorite-bearing rocks, Khanneshin carbonatite complex, Afghanistan. *A*, Hand-specimen of a fluorite- and khanneshite-bearing carbonatite dike (RT-10K-3) that has

intruded discordantly across the layering of the volcanic tuff (alvikite). *B*, Close-up of the fluorine-rich dike, showing modal fluorite and abundant yellow-colored prismatic crystals of rare earth element (REE) carbonate. *C*, Gray-toned backscattered electron image of sample RT-10K-3 in *B*: bastnäsite-(Ce) (bas), calcite (cc), calkinsite-(Ce) (cal), celestine (cel), dolomite (dol), khanneshite-(Ce) (kh). Khanneshite-(Ce) appears to have crystallized as an idiomorphic phenocryst, surrounded by interstitial dolomite and calcite, and bastnäsite-(Ce) and calkinsite-(Ce) are late alteration minerals of khanneshite-(Ce), dolomite, and calcite. *D*, Slab of a fluorite-bearing rock, Khanneshin complex. Note the banded nature of this rock, which is extraordinarily rich in barite and strontianite. Images *E* and *F* are located on the slab. *E*, False-colored backscattered electron image: barite (ba), dolomite (dol), fluorite (fl), siderite (sid), strontianite (str), and synchysite-(Ce) (syn). Igneous phenocrysts of siderite-dolomite and fluorite together with interstitial strontianite and barite. Very late crystallization of synchysite-(Ce) as an interstitial phase or immiscible droplet. *F*, False-colored backscattered electron image: barite (ba), biotite (bio), calcite (cc), dolomite (dol), fluorite (fl), strontianite (str), synchysite-(Ce) (syn), and a Li-F mica taeniolite (tae) [$KLiMg_2Si_4O_{10}F_2$]. Early crystallization of dolomite, taeniolite, and fluorite, with late interstitial crystallization of barite, strontianite, calcite, and synchysite-(Ce).

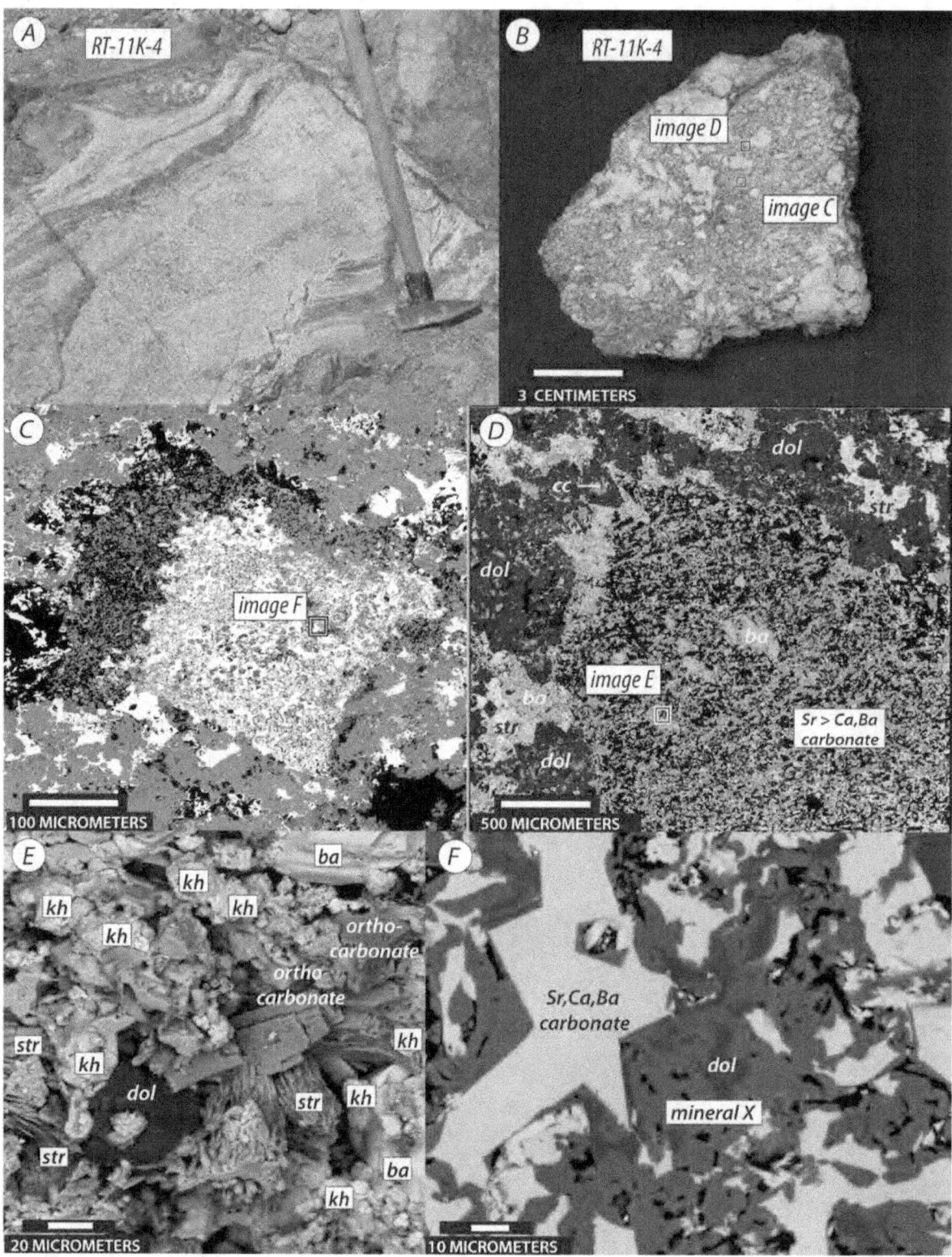

Figure 13. Mineralogy and crystallization sequence of the fluorine-rich intrusive dikes, Khanneshin carbonatite complex, Afghanistan. *A*, Outcrop of intrusive dike RT-11K-4. *B*, Slab of the fluorine-rich carbonatite dike at RT-11K-4 showing the large yellow-weathering phenocrysts of rare earth element (REE) carbonate in a fine-grained

38

matrix of dolomite, barite, strontianite, and calcite. Approximate location of images *C* and *D* are shown by inset boxes. *C*, Gray-toned backscattered electron image showing a isometric phenocryst of fluorite (?) pseudomorphed by a Sr-rich orthocarbonate and an unidentified mineral, perhaps isostructural with neighborite ($NaMgF_3$), rich in K, Ma, and F. Note location of image *F*. *D*, False-colored backscattered electron image, the yellow-colored "phenocrysts" in the intrusive dike. The yellow-colored "phenocrysts" are actually a complex aggregate of Sr-rich orthocarbonate, barite, strontianite, dolomite, and khanneshite. Note location of image *E*. *E*, Gray-toned backscattered electron image showing the fine-grained intergrowths of dolomite, barite, Sr-rich orthocarbonate, strontianite, and khanneshite. *F*, Gray-toned backscattered electron image showing fluorite pseudomorphed by a Sr-rich orthocarbonate, dolomite, and an unknown K-Mg fluoride mineral, perhaps isostructural with neighborite ($NaMgF_3$).

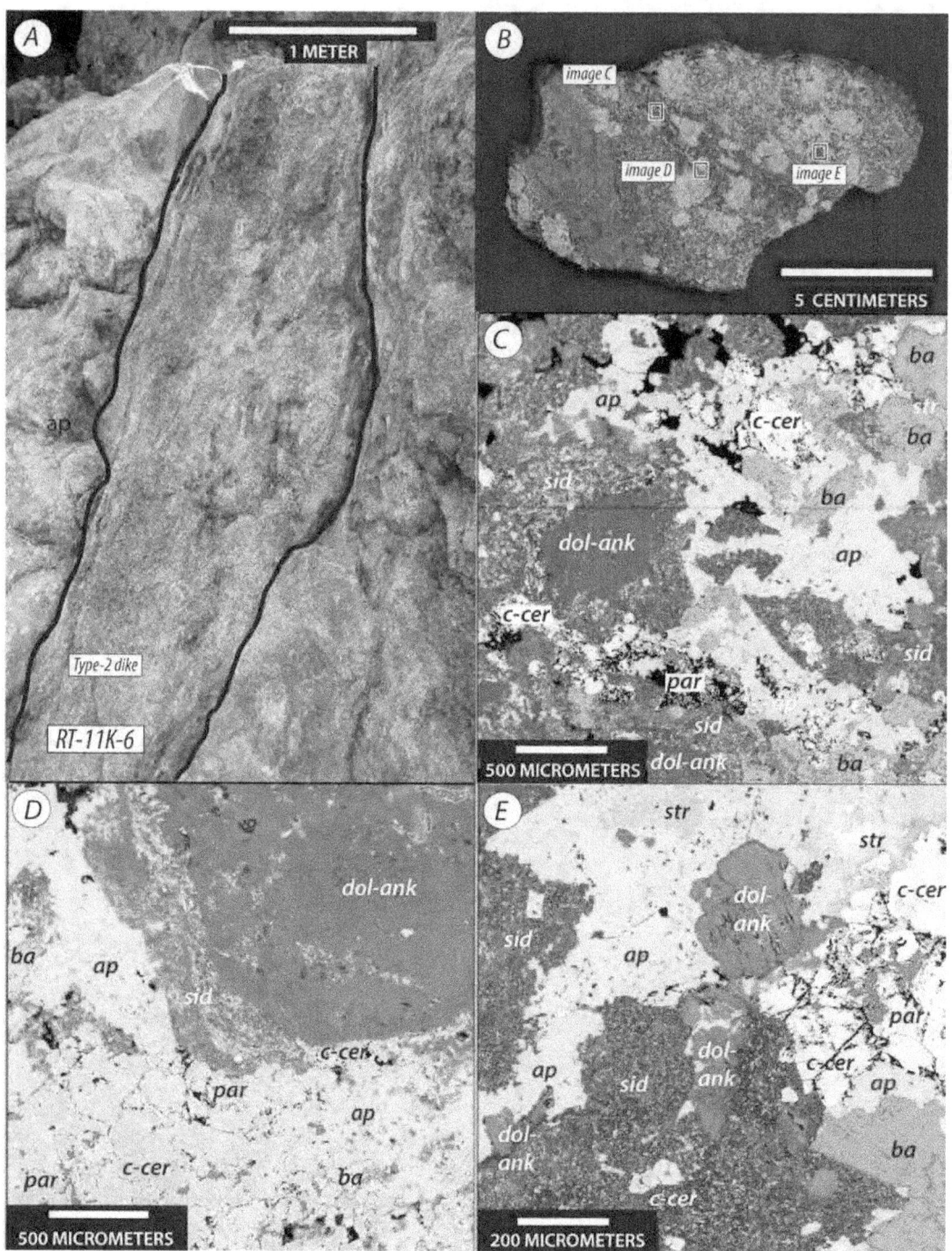

Figure 14. Mineralogy and crystallization sequence of the apatite-rich intrusive dikes, Khanneshin carbonatite complex, Afghanistan. *A*, Outcrop of intrusive dike RT-11K-6. *B*, Rock slab of sample RT-11K-6 showing the phenocrysts of carbocernaite in a matrix of dolomitic-ankerite, siderite, apatite, and barite. Location of false-colored backscattered electron images *C*, *D*, and *E* are shown as inset boxes. *C*, False-colored backscattered electron image showing the textural relationships among carbocernaite (c-cer), dolomite-ankerite (dol-ank), apatite (ap), siderite (sid), barite (ba), and parisite-(Ce) (par). Dolomitic ankerite, with siderite rims, and carbocernaite form early phenocrysts; apatite and barite form interstitial minerals; and parisite-(Ce) forms a late alteration mineral of

carbocernaite. *D*, False-colored backscattered electron image showing the textural relationships among carbocernaite (c-cer), dolomite-ankerite (dol-ank), siderite (sid), barite (ba), and apatite (ap). Dolomitic ankerite, with siderite rims, and carbocernaite form early phenocrysts; apatite and barite form interstitial minerals; and parisite-(Ce) forms a late alteration mineral of carbocernaite. *E*, False-colored backscattered electron image showing the textural relationships among carbocernaite (c-cer), dolomite-ankerite (dol-ank), siderite (sid), barite (ba), strontianite (str), apatite (ap), and parisite-(Ce) (par). Dolomitic ankerite, with siderite rims, and carbocernaite form early phenocrysts; apatite, barite, and strontianite form interstitial minerals; parisite-(Ce) forms a late alteration mineral of carbocernaite.

3.4 Structural Control on Alkaline Igneous Magmatism and LREE Mineralization

Regional fault structures played a role in locating the Khanneshin carbonatite complex. The Helmand block is bounded by two major wrench faults, the Chaman fault to the east, and the Har-i Rod fault to the north (fig. 1*A*). The north-south-striking Chaman fault has a near-vertical dip with a right-lateral sense of displacement, and it is considered by Auden (1974) to be the transform fault that bounds the northwest edge of the Indian Plate. The east-west-striking Har-i Rod fault system is a steeply dipping fault with a right lateral sense of displacement, and it is considered by Wheeler and others (2005) to form the northern boundary of the Helmand block. Thus, in a regional sense, the Helmand block is undergoing displacement to the southwest as the Indian Plate is thrust northward beneath southern Asia. Other faults within the Helmand block—for example, the Farah fault (fig. 1*A*)—are subparallel to the Har-i Rod fault, but they do not exhibit displacements as great as the Har-i Rod or Chaman faults. It is likely, therefore, that displacement is not uniform throughout the Helmand block and that some internal parts of it are in relative transtension or even pure extension.

Displacement on the Chaman and Har-i Rod faults began in Eocene time, and motion on these faults continues to the present. The Chaman fault, for example, is a principal source of earthquakes in Afghanistan (Abdullah, 1979), and a major earthquake in 1892 created a surface rupture more than 200 km long (McMahon, 1897). In addition to earthquakes, the Helmand block has experienced much intraplate volcanism. The Chagai Hills, on the southern edge of the Helmand block, contain a large field of Late Cretaceous to Eocene volcanic rocks, and other volcanic flows and sills of alkali olivine basalt both cover and intrude sedimentary strata of the Sistan basin in southeastern Iran and southwestern Afghanistan (Gansser, 1971; Lang, 1971). Perhaps the best example of an intraplate igneous field is the Kuh-i-Khwaja alkali basalt (7.3 ±0.2 million-year) (Jux and Kempf, 1983), that caps a mesa of lacustrine sediments in eastern Iran (fig. 1*A*), indicating that the Sistan depression had formed and lakes were present by latest Miocene time. This is consistent with the suggestion of Whitney (2006), who proposed that Middle to late Tertiary subsidence of basement blocks led to the formation of the Helmand basin and that continued subsidence along the Har-i Rod fault formed the Sistan basin in latest Tertiary and Quaternary time.

The most recent episode of intraplate volcanism took place in Pliocene and early Quaternary time. Three large volcanoes, Koh-i Sultan, Koh-i Taftan, and Koh-i Bazman, are located just south of the Helmand basin in neighboring Pakistan and Iran (fig. 1*A*). These Quaternary volcanic rocks intrude folded Eocene mélange and Late Cretaceous volcanic rocks, they have active thermal springs, and the present-day emission of hydrogen sulphide and sulphur dioxide gasses infers the existence of high-temperature magma at depth (Amhad and others, 2009). The Khanneshin carbonatite is the fourth alkaline igneous complex in this chain of Quaternary volcanoes (fig. 1*A*). As this trend of southwest-northeast volcanoes does not follow the surface structures of the region, it has been suggested that deep crustal fissures are responsible for their alignment (Gansser, 1971).

Faults with a northeast-southwest trend continue into Khanneshin complex. Indeed, the zone of LREE enrichment is located in the northeast margin of the intrusive vent in a section of alvikite that is bounded by north-northeast-trending faults with apparent normal displacement (graben). It is conceivable, therefore, that the fluorine- and phosphorus-rich liquids and (or) fluids that produced LREE Sr, and Ba enrichment were focused by preexisting structures that helped to channel their flow.

4.0 Estimation of LREE Resources

Mineral resources are materials in such form that economic extraction of one or more commodities is currently, or potentially, viable. We present below a preliminary assessment of potential LREE resources within the Khanneshin carbonatite complex. Our assessment is an estimation of discovered and potential LREE resources within specified volumes of rock in the marginal zone of the central vent. Because the rocks with REE enrichment have not been mapped in detail, drilled for exploration, or investigated using modern geophysical methods, our estimation is necessarily elementary with various assumptions inferred. The elementary calculation to convert rock volume to LREE resource involves converting volume to mass, using a density conversion factor, and then mass to a theoretically recoverable resource using an average grade of LREE enrichment (tables 5 and 6).

4.1 Analysis of the Soviet-Defined Zone

Soviet geologists delineated a polygonal zone (fig. 15A, B), approximately 0.64 km^2, in which ankerite-barite carbonatite is macroscopically enriched in LREE-bearing carbonate minerals. Within this zone, the total LREE contents of many rocks rise to several percent, with barite contents as much as 35 modal percent.

Table 5. Summary of barium, strontium, and light rare earth element (LREE) concentrations, barite-ankerite alvikite, Khanneshin carbonatite complex, Afghanistan.

[wt. %, weight percent; ppm, parts per million; ∑ LREE, sum of La, Ce, Pr, and Nd; Δ, average value]

Sample no.	Ba wt.%	Sr wt.%	La ppm	Ce ppm	Pr ppm	Nd ppm	Sm ppm	Eu ppm	Gd ppm	Tb ppm	Dy ppm	Ho ppm	Er ppm	Tm ppm	Yb ppm	Lu ppm	La wt.%	Ce wt.%	Pr wt.%	Nd wt.%	∑ LREE wt.%
RT-11K-1A1	19.62	3.05	10,300	14,600	1,110	2,880	258	40	109	6.9	26.4	3.4	8.3	1.01	5.8	0.86	1.030	1.460	0.111	0.288	2.889
RT-11K-1A2	21.51	3.90	11,400	15,800	1,190	3,040	267	42	115	7.5	28.4	3.6	8.5	1.06	6.1	0.91	1.140	1.580	0.119	0.304	3.143
RT-11K-1B2	18.74	3.36	10,000	14,700	1,160	3,050	278	43	109	7.7	28.7	3.5	8.4	1.02	5.7	0.88	1.000	1.470	0.116	0.305	2.891
RT-11K-2A2	19.04	2.21	5,820	8,880	840	2,740	390	75	223	27.4	124	15.8	30.5	3.03	14.3	1.64	0.580	0.888	0.084	0.274	1.826
RT-11K-2B1	20.70	3.85	8,620	11,700	1,010	3,090	415	85	271	36.5	162	20.8	40.4	3.84	17.1	2.06	0.860	1.170	0.101	0.309	2.440
RT-11K-2B2	21.01	3.64	7,980	11,200	992	3,060	417	85	267	36.2	160	20.9	39.8	3.83	16.9	2.11	0.790	1.120	0.099	0.306	2.315
RT-11K-3B31	23.63	4.43	10,400	12,200	945	2,710	445	107	367	47.5	181	18.6	30.9	2.47	11.2	1.36	1.040	1.220	0.095	0.271	2.626
RT-11K-3B32	28.57	6.05	16,000	16,600	1,180	3,040	328	65	221	27	118	13	20.7	1.72	7.1	0.81	1.600	1.660	0.118	0.304	3.682
RT-11K-4AO1	4.99	4.75	5,550	7,940	720	2,160	231	38	91.7	6.1	22.8	3.1	8.6	1.24	8.4	1.34	0.550	0.794	0.072	0.216	1.632
RT-11K-4AO2	12.92	8.24	18,800	17,600	1,170	2,770	217	34	108	6.1	23.1	3.3	8.3	1.16	7.4	1.21	1.880	1.760	0.117	0.277	4.034
RT-11K-4B3	10.63	7.05	14,500	14,500	1,020	2,540	216	34	95.8	5.7	23.1	3.4	9	1.23	7.9	1.3	1.450	1.450	0.102	0.254	3.256
RT-11K-4C1A	10.61	7.20	14,100	13,900	995	2,470	210	33	90.1	5.3	20.2	3.1	8.4	1.25	8.5	1.43	1.410	1.390	0.100	0.247	3.147
RT-11K-4C1B	3.98	1.91	1,440	2,360	244	838	189	49	166	24.4	120	18.6	44.3	5.23	27	3.53	0.144	0.236	0.024	0.084	0.488
RT-11K-5A2	24.59	2.57	5,990	13,000	1,240	3,690	507	110	349	44.1	181	19.9	32.8	2.83	12.6	1.57	0.599	1.300	0.124	0.369	2.392
RT-11K-5A3	22.44	2.91	5,870	12,400	1,190	3,580	512	112	369	47.8	201	22.3	36.7	3.29	14	1.67	0.587	1.240	0.119	0.358	2.304
RT-11K-5B1B	23.73	3.77	5,380	11,900	1,180	3,600	508	109	352	46.2	201	23.8	42.3	3.7	15.8	1.8	0.538	1.190	0.118	0.360	2.206
RT-11K-5B3B	22.79	4.95	6,400	13,300	1,270	3,990	626	136	431	55.5	236	25.5	38.2	3.01	12.7	1.52	0.640	1.330	0.127	0.399	2.496
RT-11K-5B6A	5.03	4.98	21,000	31,500	2,600	7,090	657	102	274	15.8	46.5	5	11	1.36	8.3	1.36	2.100	3.150	0.260	0.709	6.219
RT-11K-6A2A	3.25	2.37	5,790	9,030	870	2,810	397	84	279	46.4	266	43.3	98.1	9.48	40.4	4.33	0.579	0.903	0.087	0.281	1.850
RT-11K-6A2B	8.70	6.82	20,900	29,100	2,480	7,300	816	140	376	37.5	175	25.7	54.6	5.32	23.4	2.59	2.090	2.910	0.248	0.730	5.978
RT-11K-6B2	7.49	5.62	16,600	23,000	1,980	5,800	615	102	279	22.5	90.8	11.4	22	2.16	9.7	1.12	1.660	2.300	0.198	0.580	4.738
RT-11K-6B3	7.00	5.61	16,700	22,400	1,890	5,680	660	120	358	38.5	180	26.2	56	5.43	23.1	2.6	1.670	2.240	0.189	0.568	4.667

Table of summary data

	Δ Ba wt.%	Δ Sr wt.%	Δ La wt.%	Δ Ce wt.%	Δ Pr wt.%	Δ Nd wt.%	Δ LREE wt.%
Total collection	15.50	4.51	1.091	1.491	0.125	0.357	3.063
Type-1 mineralized rock (samples RT-11K-2 and -5)	19.92	3.61	0.837	1.424	0.129	0.386	2.775
Type-2 mineralized rocks (samples RT-11K-3, -4, and -6)	11.07	5.46	1.279	1.533	0.123	0.347	3.282
Fluorine-rich dike rock (RT-11K-1)	19.96	3.44	1.057	1.503	0.115	0.299	2.974

43

Table 6. Estimated light rare earth element (LREE) resources, Khanneshin carbonatite complex, Afghanistan.

[km, kilometers; g/cm³, grams per centimeter cubed; Mt, million metric tons; wt. %, weight percent; Δ, average value; --, no data]

	Length (km)	Width (km)	Depth (km)	Volume (km³)	Density (g/cm³)	Rock mass (10⁶ Mt)	Δ LREE grade (wt. %)	Mt LREE (before 10:1 dilution)[1]	Mt LREE (after 10:1 dilution)
				Zone of LREE enrichment (fig. 15)					
Type 1—Concordant veins and seams:									
Lower zone	0.750	0.550	0.150	0.061875	2.94	181.913	2.775	5.048	0.505
Upper zone	0.330	0.250	0.150	0.012375	2.94	36.383	2.775	1.010	0.101
Type-1 total				0.074250	2.94	218.295	2.775	6.058	0.606
Type 2—Discordant veins and seams[2]:									
Dike 1	0.050	0.020	0.150	0.000150	2.94	0.441	3.282	--	0.014
Dike 2	0.500	0.040	0.150	0.003000	2.94	8.820	3.282	--	0.289
Dike 3	0.400	0.035	0.150	0.002100	2.94	6.174	3.282	--	0.203
Type-2 total				0.005250	2.94	15.435	3.282	--	0.507
Total LREE enrichment[3]									1.113
				Remote-sensing polygon (fig. 15)					
NW of zone of LREE enrichment				0.071176	2.94	209.257	2.775	5.807	0.581
Within zone of LREE enrichment				0.073124	2.94	214.985	2.775	5.966	0.597
Total remote-sensing polygon									1.178

[1]Wall rock is 10 times more abundant than mineralized seams, hence 10:1 dilution factor.

[2]Estimated from mineral content in dikes, not affected by wall-rock dilution.

[3]Sum of type 1 and type 2 tonnage.

44

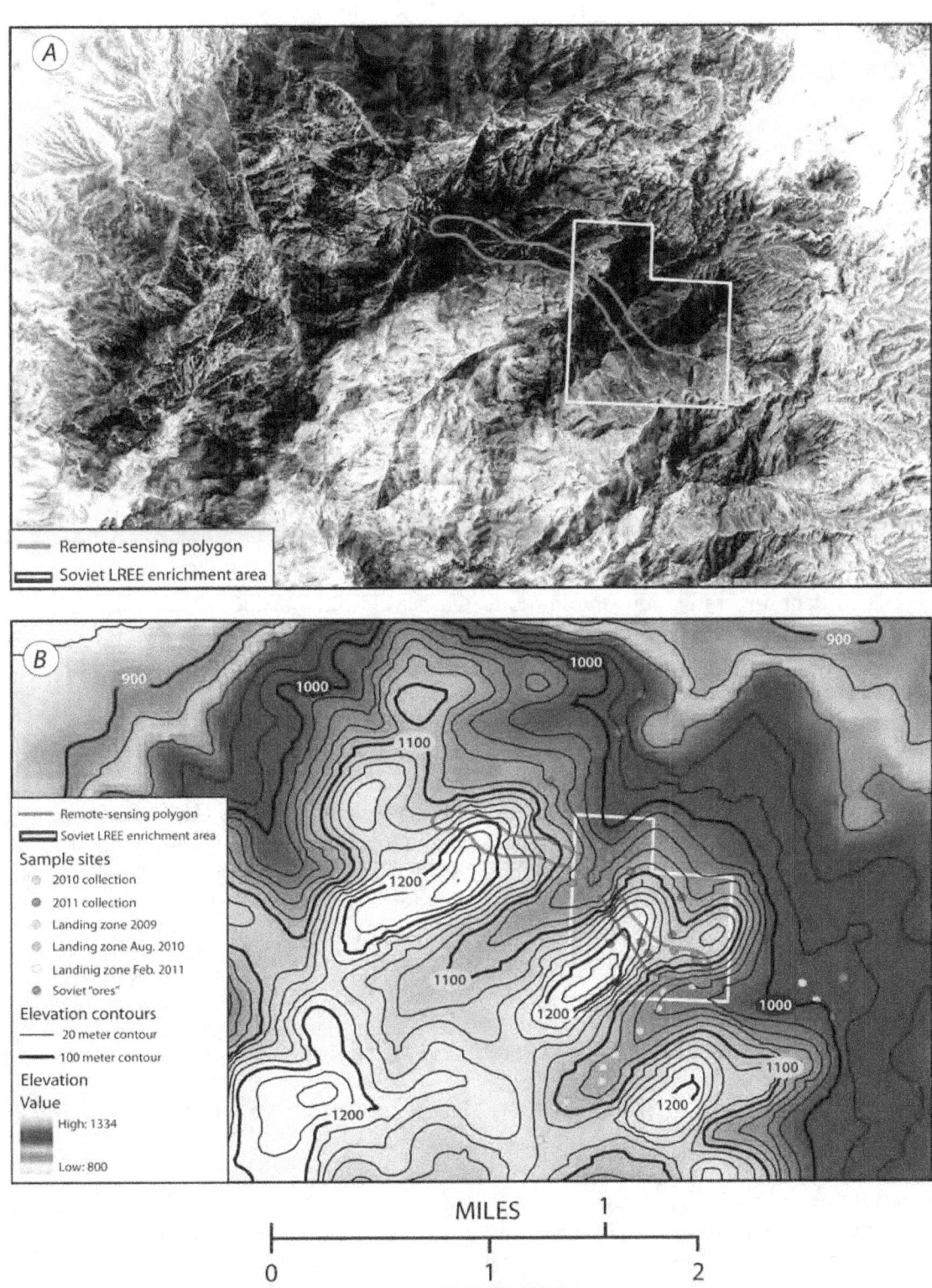

Figure 15. *A,* Area of the identified light rare earth element (LREE) prospect in the northeast part of the central intrusive vent, Khanneshin carbonatite complex, Afghanistan. The polygonal box outlined in yellow is the area of

LREE mineralization identified by Cheremitsyn and Yeremenko (1976). The polygons outlined in red are areas of distinctive rocks identified on LANDSAT images as areas of prospective LREE mineralization. *B*, Digital elevation topography of the northern part of the Khanneshin carbonatite complex. Soviet samples of "LREE ore" are indicated by the magenta dots; U.S. Geological Survey samples are indicated in red (February 2011) and green (August 2010).

Two brief excursions to the LREE-enriched zone, traverses 2 and 3 (fig. 2), mostly confirmed the work of Soviet geologists. During traverse 3 to the northern part of the LREE zone, two types of LREE mineralization were observed: (1) a concordant style of mineralization (type-1) and (2) a discordant style (type-2) in which LREE mineralization occurs within discordant tabular igneous dikes.

Concordant Layers of Mineralization.—Concordant mineralization is defined by the yellow-weathering LREE carbonates (± fluorine) that form layer-parallel, centimeter-thick bands, which alternate with dark, meter-thick layers of ankerite-barite alvikite (wall rock). On the basis of the work of Soviet scientists, whose field teams accurately described the geology and mineralogy of the entire igneous complex, we assume this style of mineralization is common throughout the area of LREE enrichment. This assumption is verified by the many samples of "REE ore" recovered and analyzed by Soviet geologists in the area and the fact that our mineralogical descriptions and whole-rock concentration data agree very well with the Soviet data. The volume of LREE mineralization, however, must be diluted by a factor of 10, which is approximately the ratio of concordantly mineralized rock to weakly mineralized wall rock (fig. 5). This dilution factor is probably a conservative value because in some sections concordant mineralization is ubiquitous, whereas in other sections the surface exposures are sparse or covered by alluvium. The proper way to determine directly this dilution factor is to drill and assay recovered rock core throughout the area of LREE enrichment. It was not possible to do this for our study because of budgetary, logistical, limited time, and security concerns.

Because drilling, core analysis, and geophysical exploration were not possible, the depth of mineralization throughout the LREE zone is estimated from ground observations. We assert a value of 150 m based on the vertical dimension of mineralized rock observed over the rugged relief of the region (~170 m). In essence, we assume a depth of mineralization that roughly mimics the surface topography of the polygonal box. This assumption is justified because the topography is young (<5 Ma), the valley walls are steep, and hence the mass of eroded rock is small relative to the unexhumed mass at depth. We believe that our estimate is conservative if, as seems likely, the zone of LREE enrichment extends to depths well beyond the arbitrary value of the local relief (fig. 15*B*). Depth of mineralization can be determined by drilling and assaying core throughout the region of known LREE enrichment.

Using an average density of mineralized carbonatite (2.94 g/cm^3), an average grade of LREE concentration (2.775 wt. percent, table 5), and a dilution factor of 10:1 (wall rock: mineral bands), we calculate that approximately 0.505 Mt of LREE is present in the concordantly mineralized rocks of the Soviet-defined zone (table 6).

Discordant Tabular Sheets.—Within the LREE-enriched zone, Soviet geologists identified more than 50 "ore bodies" of a stockwork type with widths between 60 m and 500 cm and lengths between 500 m and 20 m. The vertical dimension of the stockwork bodies is not given, but they are likely to be hundreds of meters deep because they form near-vertical dikes across the rugged relief of the region. These bodies correspond to the discordant, steeply dipping tabular sheets of this report.

Three major stockwork dikes were trenched and sampled by the Soviet teams (Cheremitsyn and Yeremenko, 1976):

1. Stockwork dike 1, located in the northwest part of LREE zone, is 20 m×50 m with a northwest strike and near vertical dip. Ten small trenches, each 2 m long, were dug across the dike. LREE

concentration (La plus Ce) for all of the Soviet samples averages more than 1.5 wt. percent (Cheremitsyn and Yeremenko, 1976).

2. Stockwork dike 2, located in the northern part of LREE zone, is 10 m to 60 m wide and 500 m long; it has a north-south strike and near-vertical dip. Three trenches were dug across the dike in its northern, central and southern part. The average concentration for La plus Ce for all of the trench samples is 1.5 wt. percent (Cheremitsyn and Yeremenko, 1976).

3. Stockwork dike 3, located in the southeast part of LREE zone, is about 35 m wide and 400 m long; it has a northeast strike and near-vertical dip. One trench across its central part wielded an average concentration for La and Ce of greater than 1.5 wt. percent (Cheremitsyn and Yeremenko, 1976).

All the Soviet analyses of the stockwork dikes yield LREE concentrations that are compatible with the average LREE concentrations of our type-2 dikes (3.282 average wt. percent $\sum$ LREE, table 5).

Our estimate of LREE resources within the discordant tabular dikes is shown in table 6. This is probably a conservative estimate because the calculation is only for the three largest dikes, and more than 50 such bodies are recognized. As with the resource calculation for the concordantly mineralized rocks, we assume the discordant dikes extend to 150 m depth and that LREE concentrations are uniform throughout the mass of rock.

Assuming an average density for carbonatite (2.94 g/cm^3) and an average grade of LREE concentration (3.282 wt. percent, table 5), we estimate approximately 0.507 Mt of LREE are present in the three largest dikes (discordant sheets) of the Soviet-defined zone of LREE enrichment (table 6).

Thus, together with the concordantly mineralized rocks, we estimate a LREE resource of approximately 1.1 Mt in the entire Soviet-defined LREE zone.

4.2 Analysis by Remote Sensing

Our complete suite of 23 samples, representing a range of rocks with both concordant and discordant REE mineralization, is greatly enriched in LREE. The average total LREE concentration for the concordantly banded rocks is 2.8 wt. percent, and the average total LREE concentration for the discordant sheets of mineralized rock is 3.3 wt. percent.

Two of the stockwork dikes, trenched and sampled by the Soviet teams, crop out in the area of our February 2011 traverse (traverse 3, fig. 2). We observed many such dikes, but we were unable to locate in the field the precise trenches sampled by the Soviet geologists. The zone of LREE enrichment is quite distinctive in the field, easily identifiable by the abundance of yellow-weathering LREE minerals, and we sought to quantify the area of LREE enrichment using remote-sensing techniques.

QuickBird satellite imagery of the area was obtained. This imagery offers relatively high spatial resolution (0.6 m for panchromatic), as well as adequate spectral resolution (red, green, blue, and near-infrared channels). The imagery of the area was pan sharpened and orthorectified to Transverse Mercator projection using ERDAS Imagine version 10 software; this software was also used for image enhancement. The imagery was then imported into ArcGIS version 9.3 for GIS analysis. Vector files of the sample sites and LREE-enriched area were created, as well as topographic contour files derived from ASTER digital terrain elevation data (DTED) for the area. Within LREE-enriched area, a polygonal area delineating the region of REE enrichment was drawn, which was based on a subjective assessment of surface color and texture. This polygon was then extended north and west beyond the Soviet-defined zone of LREE enrichment based on an objective analysis of similar image characteristics.

The revised zone of LREE-enrichment is shown in figure 15. This zone is approximately 1,490 m long, between 70 m and 150 m wide, and covers approximately 157,000 m^2. The eastern half of the polygon lies within the area of LREE enrichment delineated by Soviet geologists, and it intersects a dry stream bed where our most REE-enriched samples were collected (fig. 2). The northwestern half of the polygon lies outside the area of LREE enrichment delineated by Soviet geologists but, in our view, it includes rocks with the same spectral characteristics to those within the earlier defined LREE zone.

Using a conservative density of mineralized carbonatite (2.94 g/cm^3), an average grade of LREE concentration (2.775 wt. percent, table 5), and the same dilution factor of 10:1 (wall rock: mineral bands), we calculate an estimated LREE resource of approximately 0.581 Mt in the revised area northwest of the LREE zone and approximately 0.597 Mt in the revised area within LREE zone. By this calculation, a total LREE resource of approximately 1.178 Mt is present within the area designated as prospective by remote sensing (table 6). Although clearly preliminary, this estimate agrees well with our estimate of LREE resources within the Soviet-defined LREE zone. Both estimates comport well with the probabilistic estimate of 1.4 Mt of undiscovered REE resources in all of south Afghanistan (Peters and others 2007). In addition to LREE, the Khanneshin carbonatite is also enriched in barium (>10 wt. percent), strontium (>6 wt. percent), phosphorus (~ 2 wt. percent), and uranium (>0.05 wt. percent).

5.0 Conclusions

The Khanneshin igneous complex is unusual in many respects, but it shares some interesting characteristics in common with other carbonatites worldwide:

1. Most igneous rocks in the Khanneshin complex are varieties of carbonatite that range in composition from silico-carbonatite in the southwest part of the complex to ferro- and calico-carbonatite in the northeast part of the central vent. Only three small plugs of critically undersaturated silicate igneous rocks—leucite phonolite—are present in the southeast part of the complex.

2. Among the carbonatites at Khanneshin, the alvikites of the northeast central vent are most enriched in incompatible elements such as Ba, Sr, and LREE. These alvikites are situated within a graben (down-dropped block of rocks) whose bounding faults may have focused the emplacement of LREE-enriched magma. These LREE-enriched alvikites were emplaced unconformably above an older, and dike intruded, generation of alvikite, and thus LREE-enriched magma formed late in the petrogenetic history of the complex.

3. Two distinct styles of mineralization are present in LREE-enriched alvikites. (1) Primary igneous LREE-carbonate minerals that crystallized directly from magma (type-2) occur in igneous dikes that are as much as 60 m thick and 500 m long. (2) Secondary LREE-carbonate minerals (type-1) that were produced by metasomatic or alteration processes, perhaps involving fluid-rich immiscible liquids, occur in concordant veins and seams within the alvikite that are centimeters thick and meters long. These concordant layers are symmetrically zoned, with an inner zone rich in barite, strontianite, and apatite and outer zones rich in khanneshite-(Ce), barite, strontianite, and secondary REE minerals.

4. Type-2 igneous dikes are of two chemical types—one type is enriched in fluorine and another type is enriched in phosphorus. The fluorine-rich dikes are characterized by modal fluorite and khanneshite-(Ce) and in a single instance, an unnamed mineral, composed of K, Mg, and F, perhaps isostructural with neighborite. The phosphorus-rich rocks are characterized by modal apatite and carbocernaite, the latter forming large idiomorphic phenocrysts constituting as much as 20 modal percent of the rock. The phosphorus-rich intrusive rocks are also characterized by high Na contents (1.5 to 4.6 wt. percent Na_2O).

5. Within the type-2 igneous dikes, rich in fluorite, a proposed general sequence of LREE-Sr-Ba mineralization is:

   Sr-LREE-Ca-Na rich carbonates [khanneshite-(Ce)] → Ca-REE fluorocarbonates [bastnäsite-(Ce)] → Ca-LREE hydrated carbonate [calkinsite-(Ce)]

6. Within the type-2 igneous rocks, rich in apatite, a proposed general sequence for LREE-Sr-Ba mineralization is:

   Sr-LREE-Ca-Na rich carbonates (carbocernaite) → Ca-LREE fluorocarbonates [parisite-(Ce)] → Sr-LREE hydrated carbonate [ancylite-(Ce)]

7. All the type-1 concordantly mineralized rocks are rich in apatite and free of fluorite. The concordant bands are defined by a dark central layer of ankeritic dolomite and siderite, with interstitial barite strontianite, apatite and calcite. Khanneshite-(Ce), barite, and strontianite form the outer light colored bands. These minerals commonly display a brecciated texture within the ankerite-barite alvikite, which suggests that a LREE, Sr, and Ba-rich fluid (or liquid), perhaps a hydrothermal fluid rich in phosphorus, was introduced into the ankerite-barite alvikite late in the petrogenetic history. In many instances khanneshite-(Ce) forms spherical aggregates, approximately 100 micrometers in diameter, suggesting that it crystallized as immiscible LREE-enriched droplets. Synchysite-(Ce) and parisite-(Ce) are the common replacement minerals of khanneshite-(Ce).

8. We estimate that at least 1 Mt of light rare-earth elements (LREE) exist within the Khanneshin carbonatite, Helmand Province, Afghanistan. This newest evaluation of resources agrees well with an earlier USGS estimate of undiscovered resources in south Afghanistan (Peters and others, 2007), and it verifies the unpublished work of Soviet scientists in the 1970s (Cheremitsyn and Yeremenko, 1976; Chmyrev, 1976; Yeremenko, 1975).

The REE prospect contains total concentrations of lanthanum, cerium, praseodymium, and neodymium, ranging from 0.5 to 6.2 wt. percent, which are present in carbonate and fluorocarbonate minerals that formed during the late stages of carbonatite emplacement. The primary area of mineralization, first identified by Soviet geologists in the 1970s, covers about 0.74 square kilometers and includes both concordantly banded type-1 zones of LREE mineralization (average total LREE of 2.8 wt. percent), as well as type-2 igneous dikes that are tens of meters wide and hundreds of meters long (average total LREE of 3.3 wt. percent). The LREE prospect is comparable in grade to the world-class deposits of Mountain Pass and Bayan Obo, both LREE deposits. In addition to high concentrations of LREE, the carbonatite is greatly enriched in barium (>10 wt. percent), strontium (>6 wt. percent), phosphorus (~ 2 wt. percent), and uranium (0.05 wt. percent).

The new REE assessment evaluation is part of a larger report to be released for the TFBSO in September 2011 (Peters and others, 2011). That forthcoming report will include an updated evaluation of Afghanistan's principal deposits of gold, silver, iron, copper, lead, zinc, phosphorus, and uranium. Mineral and energy resources represent a significant source of Afghanistan's wealth, and REE are a particularly strategic and valuable commodity within their growing list of mineral resources.

6.0 References Cited

Abdullah, Shareq, 1979, The Chaman-Moqur fault: Tectonophysics, v. 52, p. 345–346.

Abdullah, S.H., Chmyriov, V.M., Stazhilo-Alekseyev, K.F., Dronov, V.I., Gannan, P.J., Rossovskiy, L.N., Kafarskiy, A.Kh., and Malyarov, E.P., 1977, Mineral resources of Afghanistan (2d ed.): Kabul, Afghanistan, Republic of Afghanistan Geological and Mineral Survey, 419 p.

Alkhazov, V.Yu, Atakishiyev, Z.M., and Azimi, N.A., 1978, Geology and mineral resources of the early Quaternary Khanneshin carbonatite volcano (southern Afghanistan): International Geology Review, v. 20, no. 3, p. 281–285.

Amhad, M., Rafiq, M., Iqbal, N., Rafique, M., and Fazil, M., 2009, Investigation of origin, subsurface processes and reservoir temperature of geothermal springs around Koh-i-Sultan volcano, Chagai, Pakistan: Pakistan Institute of Nuclear Science and Technology Report 210, 25 p.

Auden, J.B., 1974, Afghanistan-West Pakistan, *in* Spencer, A.M., ed., Mesozoic-Cenozoic orogenic belts: Geological Society of London, p. 235–253.

Castor, S.B., 2008, The Mountain Pass rare-earth carbonatite and associated ultrapotassic rocks, California: The Canadian Mineralogist, v. 46, p. 779–806.

Cheremitsyn, V.G., and Yeremenko, G.K., 1976, Report of the Hanneshin crew on the results of prospecting and evaluational activity for 1976 [in Russian]: Kabul, Afghanistan, Afghanistan Geological Survey Report 1142, 84 p., 7 pl, scale 1:10,000.

Chmyrev, V.M., 1976, Report of the Nuristan crew on the results of geological prospecting for solid commercial mineral deposits in Afghanistan, 1975 [in Russian]: Kabul, Afghanistan, Afghanistan Geological Survey Report 1028, section B, no. 5, p. 92–103.

Gansser, Augusto, 1971, The Taftan volcano (SE Iran): Ecologae Geologicae Helvetiaev, v. 64, no. 2, p. 319–334.

Jux, Ulrich, and Kempf, K.E., 1983, Regional geology of Afghan Sistan, *in* Tosi, M., ed., Prehistoric Sistan: Rome, Istituto Italiano per il Medio ed Estremo Oriente Reports and Memoirs, v. 19, p. 5–60.

Krumsiek, Klaus, 1980, Zur plattentectonischen Entwicklung des Indo-Iranischen Raumes (Resultate palaomagnetischer Untersuchungen in Afghanistan): Stuttgart, Geotektonische Forschungen Band 60, 223 p.

Lang, H.O., 1971, Uber das Jungtertiar und Quartar in sud-Afghanistan: Beihefte zum Geologischen Jahrbuch, v. 96, p. 167–208.

Long, K.R., Van Gosen, B.S., Foley, N.K., and Cordier, Daniel, 2010, The principal rare earth elements deposits of the United States—A summary of domestic deposits and a global perspective: U.S. Geological Survey Scientific Investigations Report 2010-5200, 96 p., available at *http://pubs.usgs.gov/sir/2010/5220/*.

McMahon, A.H., 1897, The southern borderlands of Afghanistan: Journal of the Royal Geographical Society, v. 19, p. 931–934.

Nakamura, N., 1974, Determination of REE, Ba, Fe, Mg, Na and K in carbonaceous and ordinary chondrites: Geochimica et Cosmochimica Acta, v. 38, no. 5, p. 757–775.

Peters, S.G., King, T.V.V , Mack, T.J ., Chornack, M.P., (eds..), Tucker, R.D.,Mossotti, V.G.,.,, Finn, R.C.A., Abraham, J.D., Kalaly, Siddiq, Bracewell, Jenifer, Stettner, Will, Chirico, P.G., Moran, Thomas, Johnson, Mikki, Hubbard, B.E., Anderson, E.D., Drenth, B.J., Kucks, R.P., Lindsay, C.R., Phillips, J.D., Sweeney, R.E., Kokaly, R.F., Hoefen, T.M., Livo, K.E., Dudek, Kay, and Theodore, T.G., 2011, Summaries of important areas for mineral investment and production opportunities of nonfuel minerals in Afghanistan: U.S. Geological Survey Open-File Report 2011–1204, available at *http://pubs.usgs.gov/of/2011/1204/*.

Peters, S.G., Ludington, S.D., Orris, G.J., Sutphin, D.M., Bliss, J.D., and Rytuba, J.J., eds., and the U.S. Geological Survey-Afghanistan Ministry of Mines Joint Mineral Resource Assessment Team, 2007, Preliminary non-fuel mineral resource assessment of Afghanistan: U.S. Geological Survey Open-File Report 2007–1214, 810 p., 1 CD–ROM, accessed August 8, 2011, at *http://pubs.usgs.gov/of/2007/1214/*.

Srivastava, R.K., 1993, Chemical classification of silica rich carbonatites: Indian Journal of Geochemistry, v. 8, p. 15–24.

Sweeney, R.E., Kucks, R.P., Hill, P.L., and Finn, C.A., 2006, Aeromagnetic and gravity surveys in Afghanistan—A web site for distribution of data: U.S. Geological Survey Open-File Report 2006–1204, accessed August 8, 2011, *http://pubs.usgs.gov/of/2006/1204/*.

U.S. Geological Survey, 2011, Mineral commodity summaries 2011: U.S. Geological Survey, 198 p., available at *http://minerals.usgs.gov/minerals/pubs/mcs/*.

Vikhter, B.Ya., Yeremenko, G.K., and Chmyrev, V.M., 1976, A young volcanogenic carbonatite complex in Afghanistan: International Geology Review, v. 18, no.11, 1305–1312 p.

Vikhter, B. Ya., Yeremenko, G.K., Chmyrev, V.M., and Abdulla, D., 1978, Pliocene-Quaternary volcanism of Afghanistan: International Geology Review, v. 20, no. 5, 525–536 p.

Wheeler, R.L., Bufe, C.G., Johnson, M.L., and Dart, R.L., 2005, Seismotectonic map of Afghanistan, with annotated bibliography: U.S. Geological Survey Open-File Report 2005–1264, 31 p., accessed August 8, 2011, at *http://pubs.usgs.gov/of/2005/1264/*.

Whitney, J.W., 2006, Geology, water, and wind in the lower Helmand Basin, southern Afghanistan: U.S. Geological Survey Scientific Investigations Report 2006–5182, 40 p., accessed August 8, 2011, at *http://pubs.usgs.gov/sir/2006/5182/*.

Woolley, A.R., and Kempe, D.R.C., 1989, Carbonatites: Nomenclature, average chemical compositions, and element distributions, *in* Bell, Keith, ed., Carbonatites—Genesis and evolution: London, Unwin Hyman, p. 1–14.

Yang, X-Y., Sun, W-D., Zhang, Y-X., and Zheng, Y-F., 2009, Geochemical constraints on the genesis of the Bayan Obo Fe-Nb-REE deposit in Inner Mongolia, China: Geochemica et Cosmochemica Acta, v. 73, p. 1417–1435.

Yeremenko, G.K., 1975, Brief characteristics of the Khanneshin carbonatite paleovolcano [in Russian]: Kabul, Afghanistan, Afghanistan Geological Survey Report 1322, 14 p., 1 pl., scale 1:10,000.

Yuan, Zhongxin, Bai, Ge, Wu, Chenyu, Zhang, Zhonguin, and Ye, Xianjiang, 1992, Geological features and genesis of the Bayan Obo REE ore deposit, Inner Mongolia, China: Applied Geochemistry, v. 7, p. 429–442.

www.ingramcontent.com/pod-product-compliance
Lightning Source LLC
Chambersburg PA
CBHW080445290526
45791CB00008BA/2618

* 9 7 8 1 4 9 7 4 6 6 6 3 0 *